BANDITS!

Pictorial History of American
Adversarial Aircraft

Dave Parsons
Derek Nelson

Motorbooks International
Publishers & Wholesalers

First published in 1993 by Motorbooks International Publishers & Wholesalers, PO Box 2, 729 Prospect Avenue, Osceola, WI 54020 USA

Motorbooks International books are also available at discounts in bulk quantity for industrial or sales-promotional use. For details write to Special Sales Manager at the Publisher's address

Library of Congress Cataloging-in-Publication Data

Parsons, Dave.
    Bandits!: pictorial history of American adversary aircraft/Dave Parsons, Derek Nelson.
    p. cm.
    Includes index.
    ISBN 0-87938-623-1
    1. Fighter planes —United States. 2. United States. Air Force. 3. United States. Navy—Aviation. I. Nelson, Derek. II. Title.
UG1242.F5P37   1993
358.4'36'0973—dc20   92-43457

Printed and bound in Hong Kong

On the front cover: Marine Adversary F-5Es glide like sharks through the deep blue. *Katsuhiko Tokunaga/Check Six*

On the back cover: Top, Air Force F-5E Aggressors. *George Hall/Check Six*. Left, a Topgun F-16N shoots into the vertical with an F-14. *Bob Lawson*. Center right, VFA-127 was the first squadron to operate the F/A-18 Hornet as an Adversary. *Michael Grove*. Lower right, a Topgun F-14 painted in Iranian Air Force markings. *Dave Parsons*

On the frontispiece: An F-5, an F-15, and an A-4 bank over the Nellis range. *George Hall/Check Six*

On the title page: A Navy F-5 flies with two Air Force F-15s. *LCdr. Dave Baranek*

Contents

Chapter 1

History of Dissimilar Air Combat Training, 1915–1945

During World War I, the American "Ace of Aces," Eddie Rickenbacker, had to fly Nieuport scouts cast off by the French when he first went into combat with the famed 94th Aero Squadron, the "Hat-in-the-Ring" squadron. Initially, the aircraft had no machine guns, which forced Raoul Lufbery to fly unarmed on the squadron's first mission against the deadly, Spandau-machine-gun-equipped Fokkers. As World War II engulfed the globe, the Japanese Zero enjoyed nearly absolute superiority over US fighters in the early days in the Pacific theater. In Korea, American fighters were bounced by the superior MiG-15 fighter. In each of these conflicts, the Air Force had to expand its fighter units and gain experience while battling superior enemy aircraft before aircraft with sufficient performance could be fielded. In Vietnam, even though the US forces had better

Lt. Edward "Butch" O'Hare after the Battle of Coral sea in which he downed five Japanese aircraft in a single sortie, earning the Medal of Honor. His aerial gunnery skills had been developed under the tutelage of LCdr. Jimmy Thach, whom O'Hare helped to develop and test the maneuver eventually known as the Thach Weave that helped counter the superiority of the Zero by use of dissimilar tactics. US Navy

aircraft, the aircrews were not trained to exploit their aircraft's strengths against the widely dissimilar performance of the MiG-17 and MiG-21. At the beginning of each of these major conflicts, the US Navy and Air Force (and its predecessors, the Army Signal Corps, Army Air Corps, and Army Air Force) found themselves facing opponents flying aircraft of dissimilar performance—and with aircrews completely unprepared to fight against these aircraft.

A notable exception was the famed American Volunteer Group (AVG) which, although not a part of the Army Air Force, flew the same P-40 into combat, yet prevailed as the only notable success against the Japanese in the first six months of the war. Its leader, Claire Chennault, had been forced into retirement as a captain partially due to his advocating of tactical thought not in concert with the prevailing bomber mentality. Chennault was hired by the Chinese government as an aviation advisor. He flew their fighters and played a primary role in assembling an air defense against the onslaught of the Japanese. He saw firsthand how the tremendous maneuverability of the Japanese fighters could not be countered by existing western aircraft. He formulated dissimilar tactics to deal with this and

saw vindication as his Flying Tigers ripped into the best of the Japanese attempts to annihilate his tiny fighter force. The idea of dissimilar air combat was unorthodox, but Chennault made believers of his pilots. The tactics worked. Eventually, Chennault was able to compare performance of his P-40s against captured Japanese aircraft.

Thousands of miles from Chennault, another legendary tactician, LCdr. Jimmy Thach, commanding officer (CO) of Fighter Squadron Three (VF-3), was disturbed when he read the *Fleet Air Tactical Unit Bulletin* of 22 September 1941. Like Chennault, Thach reasoned that it was inevitable he would have to face Japanese pilots in combat. He was searching for any information on Japanese fighter pilots and their tactics and aircraft. The bulletin confirmed what initial reports coming out of China in late 1940 had said concerning the performance of the still mysterious Japanese Zero fighter. War clouds loomed on the horizon and it was obvious that it was only a matter of time before his F4F Wildcats would have to take on this clearly superior fighter. Since taking command, he had molded his squadron into crack shots and superior airmen. Yet, he realized that even if the Zero's performance was half as good as the reports

Flight deck of the Japanese aircraft carrier Kiryu on 7 December 1941 as aircraft, including the still mysterious Zero fighter, prepare to launch their infamous attack on Pearl Harbor. At the time, the Zero had over a year of combat against the Chinese and had yet to suffer a loss in air-to-air combat. The Zero had a clear margin of superiority against the latest Allied aircraft and became the symbol of the Japanese offensive in the Pacific. US Navy

Thach and O'Hare, in their Fighting Three F4F Wildcats in April 1942 just prior to the combat test of the Thach Weave in the Battle of Midway. National Archives

said, his F4F Wildcats would be a severe disadvantage no matter how good his pilots were. Conventional tactics wouldn't be able to counter the speed, climb, and turning performance of the Zero. He began to devise a tactic to counter the aerodynamic performance superiority of the Zero. Working at night on his kitchen table with match sticks simulating the two fighters, he devised a weaving tactic that became known as the Thach Weave.

Thach realized that to test his theories in the air he needed a dissimilar opponent that would simulate the relative differences of performance between the Wildcat and the Zero. As no aircraft in the United States had performance even close to the Zero, he improvised, as he later recalled in the book *The Pacific War Remembered* by John T. Mason, Jr., published by Naval Institute Press: "'We [had] to practice this, but who's going to be the Zeros? How are we going to find airplanes of that sort, that fast and with that high a performance?....I told Lt. (jg) Edward 'Butch' O'Hare to take four aircraft and use full power. I would take four and put a little mark on the throttle quadrant and never advance it more than halfway.'"

Prior to the epic Battle of Midway, Thach found himself in Hawaii stripped of his veteran pilots who were used to flesh out other squadrons. He was faced with the daunting task of taking brand-new ensigns into combat with scant time to train them in aerial gunnery let alone his new tactic. He conducted a rigorous training program out of the base at Kaneohe and was able to instruct at least some of the pilots he would lead at Midway in the Thatch Weave. Thach had the satisfaction of seeing his tactic work in the battle. His improvised in-house dissimilar air combat had been crucial in validating his tactic and undoubtedly saved the lives of at least several junior pilots. It was a big edge for the Wildcat pilots in World War II and has been used by American pilots as recently as the Vietnam war when Navy pilots of prop-driven A-1 Skyraider used a version of the Thach Weave in 1965 when they were jumped by a North Vietnamese Air Force (NVAF) MiG-17 jet. They shot it down.

Ever since Thach realized the utility of having an "adversary" aircraft to validate tactics and prepare his pilots for air-to-air combat, fighter training entered a new age although it would be more than twenty years before a renaissance in fighter training established dissimilar air combat training (DACT) as an integral part of fighter-aircrew training. Having dedicated Adversary (Navy) and Aggressor (Air Force) units is viewed by some as an expensive luxury and only the United States has established full-time Adversary units to train its fighter aircrews.

Many of today's aircrews take the presence of Adversary and Aggressor units for granted because DACT has been an established part of fighter training for over twenty years. Very few fighter crews are still on active duty that remember what it was like before the air-combat training renaissance that grew out of the Navy's so-called Ault Report (more on this in chapter 3). The report spawned the Navy Fighter Weapons School (Topgun), Adversary squadrons, air combat maneuvering (ACM), and the ACM range (ACMR), which is now known as tactical aircrew combat training system (TACTS) in the Navy. The Air Force followed suit with Aggressor squadrons, expansion of air-to-air training in their already established Fighter Weapons School and an ACM instrumentation (ACMI) range at Nellis Air Force Base (AFB). From 1972 on, DACT was expanded, creating additional Adversary and Aggressor units and application of the training to aircraft other than fighters. Training in ACM in various forms became more and more professional, with Adversary and Aggressor pilots merging the aspects that are part science and part art.

World War I Precedents

Ever since the first swirling dogfights of World War I, aviators became aware of the differing performance of their aircraft as compared to those of their opponents. A pilot had to first master the quirks of his own machine and be able to fly it to its limits. If he survived long enough, he then needed to learn how his machine compared to that of his opponent.

Many designs matured during the rapid evolution of aerial fighting machines in World War I. Engine technology played a crucial role as it yielded higher speeds and better climb performance. Aerodynamic design played an equally important role influencing turning ability as well as the important climb and dive performance. With so many types entering service over a short time period, each new machine could enjoy a relatively short period before its design's strong and weak points became obvious to its opponents.

The first recorded use of adversary aircraft, even though it wasn't called that in those days, was by the Germans in World War I. Initially, air machines were used for aerial spotting for artillery and reconnaissance. Their design was not for attacking other aircraft. As air machines from sides began encountering each other, aviators began devising ways to destroy their opponent's aircraft. Eventually aircraft were designed with air combat in mind. The first unit to be created solely as a fighter unit was brought together under Oswald Boelcke. Equipped with Fokker Eindecker EI monoplanes fitted with a single Spandau machine gun, Jasta 2 became the scourge of the skies on the Western Front during the summer of 1915. Boelcke and Max Immelmann made the Fokker a dreaded sight to the Allied bombing and observation aircraft.

The British and French soon fielded armed aircraft to counter Jasta 2's fighters. No. 24 Squadron Royal Air Force (RAF) was equipped with de Havilland DH2 pusher biplanes and sent to France in February of 1916 as the first Allied "fighter" unit. Between 8 April and 25 May, No. 24 squadron downed forty-four German airplanes and forced another seventeen to land.

To train his pilots to deal with this threat, Boelcke gathered captured machines that had been downed in German territory, refurbished them, and then flew them against his own pilots to show their comparative performance. As dogfights continued, more and more aircraft were brought down, many in flames, but the slow speeds resulted in some aircraft being in restorable shape, especially those in relatively controlled force landings. Both

A Marine F4F Wildcat bears the scars and victory markings of many successful encounters with Rabaul-based Zeros. Some of the top-ranking Japanese aces were flying out of Rabaul. They were infuriated and stymied at first by the use of dissimilar tactics such as the Thach Weave. Without the development of dissimilar tactics, it is doubtful that this Wildcat would have lasted to score nineteen victories. National Archives

The invincible Zero lost its mystery when an example was found in a bog in the Aleutian islands after an unsuccessful forced-landing attempt. It was subsequently salvaged, restored to flying condition, and used in an extensive evaluation against American fighters, allowing dissimilar tactics to be devised. This Zero is a later model as evidenced by the clipped wings. Jeff Ethell

sides began keeping their adversary's machines for training. A few pilots actually preferred the captured aircraft and flew them into battle.

After the war and the characteristic reduction of forces after major conflicts, fighter aircraft design continued to evolve, producing successive improvements in speed and climbing performance. During the "golden years," speed often became the primary measure of a fighter's effectiveness. Often, one design would give a pilot speed and diving advantages at the expense of turning ability. Aircraft could typically be characterized as either high-speed, quick-diving machines or tight-turning dogfighters.

In impromptu dogfights between Army and Navy fighters from nearby fields, these relative measures were quickly demonstrated. When similar aircraft within the same unit practice dogfighting, the fight tends to develop into a horizontal descending turning contest when pilots are evenly matched and the start of the fight is neutral. Most pilots felt that given the altitude advantage, they could get in a firing position behind their opponent and stay there indefinitely. Of course seasoned pilots could start from a disadvantage and turn the tables on a rookie. The problem arose when pilots met a dissimilar type aircraft, especially one that was unfamiliar.

World War II

The Chinese were the first to encounter the Japanese Zero when they first fought it in the air over Chung-King on 13 September 1940. The Zero enjoyed free rein as it was superior in almost every aspect to the generation fighters in service throughout the world. America's first team would have to face the mighty Zero in their F4F Wildcats, P-40 Warhawks, and P-39 Airacobras, none of which could fight the Zero on even terms. Only by using tactics that took advantage of their fighters' strengths and the enemy fighters' weaknesses—and by relying on the rugged construction, self-sealing fuel tanks, and armor protection of the American fighters—could the American fliers hold back the Japanese until the superior F4U Corsair, P-38 Lightning, and F6F Hellcat fighters entered the fray.

While Thach wrestled with how to defeat the Zero, Claire Chennault was implementing his plan. His solution was different than Thach's because Chennault's forces were land-based, which allowed him to establish an extremely effective early-warning system. Knowing where the Japanese formations were gave Chennault's Flying Tigers, the ability to husband their scarce fighter resources and use them most effectively. Most importantly, the early warning allowed the American fliers enough time to climb to an altitude that gave them a significant tactical advantage. Chennault preached a diving, hit-and-run attack that made the most of the P-40's one significant performance advantage over the Zero: the dive.

This tactic was most unorthodox at the time. RAF pilots stationed at Rangoon, Burma, alongside the AVG were threatened with court-martial if seen diving away from a fight. They stayed in close with their Hurricanes and Brewster Buffaloes and suffered far greater losses than the unconventional and successful AVG pilots using dissimilar tactics.

Thach didn't have to wait very long to test his tactic in combat. VF-3 flew from USS Yorktown escorting the SBD dive bombers and TBD torpedo bombers against the cream of the Japanese carrier aviation. The torpedo bombers became separated and were utterly decimated by the defending Zeros.

Thach's Wildcats were at 5,500 feet when they were attacked by fifteen to twenty Zeros. The Zeros lined up and conducted sequential attacks on the slower Wildcats making a firing run every 20–30 seconds. Thach was unable to deploy into the Weave before the attacks began, and the number 4 Wildcat was shot down as he led his flight into a hard right turn trying to spoil the attack. A Zero pulled up and passed in front of the American fighters, and Thach fired a snap shot as the Japanese fighter flashed past, setting it afire. It burst into flames.

Thach's wingman was familiar with the Weave, but the remaining pilot, Lt. (jg) Brainard Macomber, was a new arrival from VF-42 and knew nothing about it. Even worse, Macomber's radio was out so Thach led

the three ships in a line astern formation, weaving to thwart the relentless attacks of the Zeros. He then directed his wingman, Ens. Robert Dibbs, to take an abeam position as if he were leading a section and commence the Weave.

One of the Zeros, seeing an apparent breakup of the formation, made a pass on Dibbs and latched onto his tail. Dibbs radioed Thach, "Skipper, there's a Zero on my tail! Get him off!" Dibbs made a hard port turn into Thach in accordance with the Weave tactic as Thach made a corresponding starboard turn toward Dibbs. They passed close aboard with the Zero still in hot pursuit unaware of the trap laying ahead. Thach was now approaching the Zero head-on from the preferred position of being slightly below his target's flight path giving him a favorable firing position. Thach commenced firing, and his .50cal. slugs tore into the nose of the Zero, causing the engine to ignite into flames. Thach and Dibbs continued to weave forcing the Zeros to break off their attacks. Macomber flew wing on Thach wondering what Dibbs was up to and becoming highly irritated at Dibbs for breaking formation. It wasn't until return to the carrier that he found out he was part of the combat test of the Thach Weave.

The Zero pilots continued their relentless attacks responding to the Weave only occasionally by aborting their firing passes when the Weave brought them in front of the American fighters' guns. When a second Zero attempted to chase Dibbs through the turn, Thach raked its fuselage with .50cal. fire resulting in Thach's third claim for the day.

Thach's other section escorting the TBD torpedo bombers was also attacked by Zeros and forced to fight defensively all the way to the Japanese fleet. Unable to set up the Thach Weave, they did manage to score two kills and two probables.

Thach's tactic had proven itself in the face of overwhelming odds. The word quickly spread and other units adopted the tactic. Although the ultimate solution was the fielding of the F4U Corsair and the F6F Hellcat, both aircraft were still in development and would not be available until the sum-

mer of 1943. Until then, the Wildcat would remain as the Navy's front-line fighter facing the Zero. Carrier fighter complements were upped to twenty-seven and then to thirty-six Wildcats, but the Thach Weave would be their greatest asset in dealing with the Zero. Thach was recognized for his achievement by the award of the Distinguished Service Medal, a lofty award befitting his significant contribution, which undoubtedly had saved many aircraft and would continue to do so.

In late summer 1942, Marines went ashore at Guadalcanal beginning an epic struggle for that island and the whole of the Solomon Islands chain. The Japanese vigorously resisted this intrusion into their territory by launching air attacks from their fortress at Rabaul. Marines flying Wildcats from the bare-bones airfield on Guadalcanal also adopted the Thach Weave. The Japanese Zero pilots flying out of Rabaul were initially confounded by the tactic and the Marines' hit-and-run attacks.

Tadashi Nakajima was Japan's leading ace and commander of a Lae-based Zero unit that was recalled to Rabaul. One of his pilots was Saburo Sakai whose score was already approaching sixty and who was destined to be Japan's second highest scoring ace of the war and leading surviving ace. Both pilots were absolute masters of their aircraft and aerial combat. Sakai relates their reaction to the Thach Weave when they encountered Guadalcanal Wildcats using it: "For the first time Nakajima encountered what was to become a famous double-team maneuver on the part of the enemy. Two Wildcats jumped on the commander's plane. He had no trouble in getting on the tail of an enemy fighter, but never had a chance to fire before the Grumman's teammate roared at him from the side. Nakajima was raging when he got back to Rabaul; he had been forced to dive and run for safety."

Lt. "Boogie" Hoffman related the following story concerning initial use of the Weave in the book *Fighting Squadron* by Robert Winston.

"'My own division was cruising along the southeast of Roi at about four thousand feet when we saw a big bunch of Zeros, fifteen to twenty planes, diving on us from astern, dropping their belly tanks on the way down. We immediately went into a defensive weave, but there were too many of them and they knew their business too well. Each time we swung to the outside of a turn they would hit us. Each time we would weave we would get in short snap shots at them, but we were pulling so many G's in such tight turns at high speed that my guns jammed, one after another, until I had only one gun firing. The action was so violent that I couldn't relax for an instant, not even long enough to touch my hydraulic gun chargers, even with one foot.

"'We knew we were hitting them, but we couldn't take time out even to see if they flamed or splashed, for they were all over us. Then my wingman got hit. First they set one of his wing tanks afire, and then the other. Then he dropped down out of control with both wing tanks burning. He didn't get out. You feel pretty bad when you lose your wingman, and he was the best wingman I ever saw. Well, we finally worked our way back toward the ship and gradually pulled away from the yellow devils. That old Thach Weave saved our necks, beyond any doubt. If we had ever separated with that mob on our tails, not one of us would ever have gotten back.'"

The Aleutian Prize

While Thach was validating his tactic at Midway and Chennault's shark-mouthed P-40s were decimating the Japanese, another significant event occurred. Concurrent with the attack on Midway, a Japanese task force attacked the Aleutian Islands of Alaska. A Zero had been found virtually intact in 1942 on Akutan Island. Its pilot had tried to make an emergency landing on a bog after suffering battle damage during the 4 June 1942 attack on Dutch Harbor. He apparently mistook the soft bog for a hard surface and tried to land with the landing gear down. A Patrol Squadron Forty-one (VP-41) PBY Catalina spotted the Zero on 10 July 1942 lying on its back. An intensive salvage effort requiring three expeditions was able to retrieve the Zero from the remote site, and it eventually made its way to the United

States, where it was restored to flying condition. By late September it was involved in a series of flight tests and comparisons against the latest US fighters.

After the testing establishment had finished their evaluation of the rebuilt Zero, some farsighted and ambitious Navy fighter pilots succeeded in getting it released for use in San Diego. One of the pilots was RAdm. Bill Leonard (then a lieutenant) who was fighter training officer with COMFLEETAIRWESTCOAST (office of the commander of all the Navy's fleet aircraft on the West Coast). His boss at the time was the famed LCdr. James Flatley who, along with Leonard, had fought the Zero in the early months of the war in F4F Wildcats. They knew firsthand of the Zero's phenomenal maneuverability. They also knew of its weaknesses and the best way to survive and win an engagement: allow pilots to train against the real thing. They argued convincingly to secure the Zero (the existence of which was still a closely held secret) to use against fleet units in advanced stages of training just prior to deployment.

Principally, the Zero was flown as an adversary aircraft against the F6F and F4U to show the pilots "how it smelled in the air." It was also made available to squadron COs and senior pilots to fly themselves in order to acquaint them with the Zero's remarkable maneuverability. Reports were one thing, but there was nothing like seeing the real thing in living color. Leonard had seen the Zero firsthand while flying an F4F Wildcat during both the Battle of Coral Sea and Midway and could attest to its remarkable maneuverability, especially at low speeds.

Leonard used the Zero primarily against air wings in their advanced stages of training, just prior to deployment to the Pacific combat zone. He also demonstrated it to squadrons. Unfortunately, the Zero was later lost in a taxiing accident when an SB2C Helldiver didn't see the small fighter and chewed it into scrap with its propeller. A more up-to-date Zero was subsequently found as the American offensive began capturing real estate with abandoned aircraft during the island hopping campaign. This has re-

mained the first documented example of the use of an adversary aircraft in a broad training role. (Oswald Boelcke had kept the captured aircraft as squadron assets, whereas the Zero was used to train many squadrons.) The program was remarkably visionary and it presaged today's Adversary and Aggressor training.

As Leonard demonstrated, the best way to be ready for an opponent is to be able to train against his aircraft, especially if the opponent's aircraft performance is radically different from the performance of your own. Of course, it is not always possible to obtain flying examples of your potential opponents. The Zero based at North Island was only one airplane, not quite enough to train the multitude of fighter pilots under instruction during World War II.

Lt. "Boogie" Hoffman was one the pilots assigned to do initial comparative testing of the salvaged Zero and returned to Pacific combat with VF-31 where he shared his experiences. No other formal dissimilar training existed, but there were opportunities for plenty of informal encounters.

"Bouncing" Friendly Aircraft

Stateside during World War II, anything in the air was fair game. And if nothing could be found airborne, a pilot merely had to head for a neighboring field (preferably belonging to a sister service) and "beat it up" until an opponent took up the challenge. The following passage by Cdr. Bud Furney from *The Hook* magazine describes the atmosphere.

"In early 1943, the Vought F4U-1 Corsair arrived and I immediately moved into the old bird-cage model with the snap-roll. As the OTU [operational training unit] expanded, I moved to Green Cove Springs. That's about when the culprit appeared in the form of a US Army Air Corps operation at Waycross, Georgia. They had North American P-51 Mustangs and their stage of training was apparently a bit further along than ours. Part of their operation included interception of nearly every aircraft that flew near Waycross. Airliners were merely "tallyhoed" and never saw the P-51s. But it was a bit different when a Navy aircraft transited the area. Those were freer days and impromptu "battle practice" was considered good training.

"It ultimately got to where the Waycross P-51s would come down to Green Cove Springs and jump on our students. They invariably picked single Corsairs which would be guys just getting checked out. Obviously, the results were pretty one-sided and the Corsairs didn't look so hot against the Mustangs."

To redeem Navy honor and to give the Mustang pilots a taste of the Corsair's true capability, Commander Furney decided to pay a visit to Waycross. Launching on a post-maintenance check flight, he accomplished the required checks en route to Waycross. Eluding two divisions of Mustangs trying to intercept, he arrived at Waycross doing about 400 knots and then proceeded to conduct a simulated strafing attack on the base.

"P-51s were scrambling all over the place—on runways, taxiways, anywhere. It's a wonder they didn't mess up a few on the ground. Another pass and I had a bunch of P-51s trying to close on my tail. The old Corsair racked around in a turn that clearly showed the P-51s what a better airplane could do. I came in behind them and scattered them all over the place!"

Commander Furney never heard anything more about his "mission." He concluded the Army Air Corps guys were too embarrassed to have been taken by a single Corsair and it was probably viewed as a good training experience for the combat-bound Mustang pilots.

If the skies around the local base were bare, then some units took active measures to ensure that opponents would show. Cdr. Tom Blackburn, CO of the fledgling VF-17 Jolly Rogers was working his squadron up in the isolated outer banks of North Carolina at Manteo, and when he deemed his pilots ready, he sent out the following dispatch to all the squadrons in the Hampton Roads area: "'Combat' air patrol will be airborne over Manteo from 0800 until 1200 each weekday. Visitors welcome."

Blackburn got the visitors he wanted in the form of fighters, dive bombers, torpedo bombers, and even some patrol types. He commented:

Swirling contrails mark intense aerial combat as F6F Hellcats do battle with massive waves of Japanese attackers during the Battle of Philippine Sea in June 1944. Their success in what came to be known as the "Marianas Turkey Shoot" was due to the superior design of the Hellcat and lessons learned from the dissimilar tests against the Japanese Zero, which resulted in tactics that negated the advantages of the Zero. National Archives

When it first appeared, the Fw 190 proved superior to the Spitfire, so the RAF was desperate to get a flyable example to evaluate. The British were planning to raid a German aerodrome and fly out an Fw 190 when a young German pilot inadvertently landed at an RAF field in Southern England. This Fw 190 was sent on a flying tour to Allied bases along with the Bf 109 in the background for orientation and dissimilar training. Jeff Ethell

13

Allied forces captured several German fighters during advances in North Africa that overran German airfields. This Bf 109 was flown by members of the 85th Squadron, 79th Fighter Group. The Messerschmitt's fuselage was painted with wide yellow bands to mark it as a captured asset and flown in company with escorting Allied fighters. Dedicated Adversary units with surrogate aircraft weren't necessary when the real thing was available. Jeff Ethell

"I have a vivid mental picture of a section of dive-bombers pulling out of their attack on the treetops at 300-plus knots with Corsairs, wing tips skyward, making 90-degree deflection attacks at their level. We were busy. We never had more fun or better training."

Although air combat can be very debilitating, the contest between two aircraft is considered by most to be fun, at least in training. An old adage goes, "If you're not having fun, you're doing something wrong." Of course, from a different perspective, a pitched battle at low level over a town isn't all fun. Blackburn's squadron had been previously based at NAS Norfolk, right under the noses of numerous flag officers. When Ens. Ira "Ike" Kepford had a dogfight with an Army Air Force P-51 that descended below 500 feet over Norfolk, Blackburn got to have a one-way conversation with Vice Admiral Bellinger, COMNAVAIRLANT (commander of the Navy's aircraft in the Atlantic Fleet), about the antics of his "hellions." Blackburn's squadron was soon transferred to Manteo.

Fun aside, this type of training is, as Blackburn suggests, good training. Beating up a rival service's airfields and jumping its aircraft had a direct corollary with combat operations in the Pacific. The pilots flying out of Guadalcanal had to be ready to engage Zeros at any time. The landing pattern wasn't safe, nor was the take-off roll. There is sound reason behind the Navy's carrier landing technique in which aircraft maintain combat speeds until over the field, at which time the aircraft goes into a "break" turn minimizing the time at slow speeds before landing in case a marauding Zero should happen to show.

Even over wartime England, friendly Allied pilots often took each other on in chance encounters when not on combat missions. Perhaps the most famous being Col. Robert S. Johnson's mock engagement in which he pitted his P-47 Thunderbolt against an RAF Spitfire IX which he encountered by chance over the English countryside. In a classic dissimilar fight, Johnson used his zoom and diving advantage while staying away from a pure turning fight, where the Spitfire held the advantage. As recounted in his classic book, *Thunderbolt!* coauthored with Martin Caidin:

"This was going to be fun. I knew he could turn inside the heavy Thunderbolt; if I attempted to hold a tight turn the Spitfire would slip right inside me. I knew, also, that he could easily outclimb my fighter. I stayed out of those sucker traps. First rule in this kind of a fight: don't fight the way your opponent fights best. No sharp turns; don't climb; keep him at your own level.

"We were at 5,000 feet, the Spitfire skidding around hard and coming in on my tail. No use turning; he'd whip right inside me as if I were a truck loaded with cement, and snap out in firing position. Well, I had a few tricks, too. The P-47 was faster, and I threw the ship into a roll. Right here I had him. The Jug could out-roll any plane in the air, bar none. With my speed, roll was my only advantage, and I made full use of the manner in which the Thunderbolt could whirl. I kicked the Jug into a wicked left roll, horizon spinning crazily, once, twice, into a third. As he turned to the left to follow, I tramped down on the right rudder, banged the stick over to the right. Around and around we went, left, right, left, right. I could whip through better than two rolls before the Spitfire even completed his first. And this killed his ability to turn inside me. I just refused to turn. Every time he tried to follow me in a roll, I flashed away to the opposite side, opening the gap between our two planes.

"Then I played the trump. The Spitfire was clawing wildly through the air, trying to follow me in a roll, when I dropped the nose. The Thunderbolt howled and ran for earth. Barely had the Spitfire started to follow—and I was a long way ahead of him by now—when I jerked back on the stick and threw the Jug into a zoom climb. In a straight or turning climb, the British ship had the advantage. But coming out of a dive, there's not a British or a German fighter that can come close to a Thunderbolt rushing upward in a zoom. Before the Spit pilot knew what had happened, I was high above him, the Thunderbolt hammering around. And that was it—for in the next few moments the Spit flier was amazed to see a less maneuverable, slower-climbing Thunderbolt rushing straight at him, eight guns pointed ominously at his cockpit."

Johnson knew the strong points of his aircraft and, even more importantly, how they could be used to an advantage against an opponent with dissimilar performance. He evidently used this to great advantage against his German adversaries as he finished his tour with twenty-eight victories tying him for first place in the European Theater among US Army Air Forces pilots.

Flying Captured Aircraft in Europe and Africa

Johnson wasn't the only one curious about the performance of the Spitfire. The Germans were particularly anxious to get their hands on the latest version with the improved engine that was on par with the Fw 190. The first Spitfire versus Bf 109 duel occurred on 23 May 1940 over France where the CO of No. 74 Squadron had force-landed with a damaged engine. During an attempt to rescue the CO with a two-seat Miles Master, escorting Spitfires from No. 54 Squadron engaged several Bf 109s attempting to strafe the Miles Master as it landed. Pilot Officer Alan Deere intercepted a Bf 109 in its strafing run and downed it, and then proceeded to chase off two more Bf 109s. A Spitfire was now down in German occupied territory. The British were equally anxious to get their hands on a Bf 109. They didn't have to wait long. By June, a crash-landed Bf 109 was being evaluated at Farnborough.

When the Fw 190 showed up in 1941, handily downing three Spitfire Vs in its combat debut on September 1, the RAF was hard pressed to counter this superlative German fighter. Even the Spitfire Vb that gained superiority over the Bf 109E and F variants could not best the Fw 190. Plans were drawn up to raid a German airfield and fly an example to England for evaluation. Before this occurred, the British were delighted when an Fw 190A-3 landed in England by mistake in June 1942. After evaluation, the Fw 190 was flown to various Allied bases in England along with a Bf 109 to acquaint pilots with the aircraft. As they captured German airfields in North Africa, Allied forces eventually captured German aircraft. These were painted in garish colors to prevent friendly forces from mistaking them for German-flown aircraft and used to train Allied pilots about their performance dissimilarities and to practice tactics.

Interestingly, when the British and Germans evaluated the Bf 109 and Spitfire, respectively, both opponents decided after careful examination that their own aircraft was superior to that of their enemy—mostly because each side favored different performance attributes.

The Germans had an ambitious dissimilar aircraft training program formed around captured Allied aircraft. Under command of Flugkapitan Rosarius, this unit came to be known as Beutezirkus Rosarius (Rosarius Captured Aircraft Circus). Based at Oranienburg near Berlin, the unit received Allied aircraft after flying performance and other characteristics were evaluated by the Beutereferat (Department for Captured Aircraft) at the Luftwaffe Test Center at Rechlin. The Beutezirkus visited various Luftwaffe bases to give pilots a firsthand look at Allied aircraft, much like the Allies did with captured Axis aircraft. Additionally, COs were given a chance to fly the aircraft for themselves.

The Beutezirkus acquired a P-47D-2 after it force-landed near Caen, France, intact in 1943. German fighter pilots were most anxious to have a close look at this fighter legendary for its speed. In his book, *Luftwaffe Test Pilot: Flying Captured Allied Aircraft of World War 2*, published by Jane's, Hans-Werner Lerche, head of the Beutereferat, recalls that when he arrived at Caen to pick the Thunderbolt, a highly decorated fighter ace had flown into Caen in his Bf 109 from the nearby base at Cormeilles in hopes of flying the Thunderbolt:

"Our fighter ace had flown to Caen in his Bf 109 and naturally did not want to miss the opportunity of flying back to his operational base at the controls of the Thunderbolt. Apart from the fact that I had orders to make the first flight anyway, I had the impression that his enthusiasm had waned somewhat by the sight of so many unknown instruments and levers."

Throughout the vast aerial battlefields of World War II, the tactics that proved successful were those that were based on the dissimilar performance of the combatants' aircraft—even though the term "dissimilar air combat" was still decades away from being institutionalized. Whether pilots realized it or not, the informal bouncing of friendly aircraft provided the dissimilar opponents needed to hone air-to-air combat skills. In every theater, opponents placed high priority on capture of opposing aircraft for exploitation and comparative tests in which dissimilar tactics were devised. Both Allied and Axis air forces developed specialized units to provide dissimilar air combat training after capturing sufficient examples of their opponent's aircraft. In the post war stand down, the utility of such units did not lead to formalized dissimilar air combat training although informal bouncing remained as popular as ever.

Chapter 2

US Air Force Dissimilar Air Combat Training

The F-86 was rushed into service in Korea to deal with the MiG-15 threat. Many veteran pilots from World War II had a chance to discover the relative performance between the two swept-wing fighters, which were quite similar in appearance, but had differences in handling, top speed, dive speed, and ceiling.

The US forces desperately tried to obtain a MiG-15 for comparative testing with the Sabre—going so far as to offer a $100,000 reward to any North Korean, Chinese, or Soviet pilot who would defect with a MiG-15—but that didn't happen until North Korean Lt. Kim Su Nok defected just after the armistice was declared with his MiG-15B.

Even though the F-86 and MiG-15 were quite similar in appearance, there were enough dissimilar performance characteristics that dissimilar tactics were devised. Sabre pilots knew their control system was superior especially in transonic fighting and they could catch a MiG-15 in a dive, but they couldn't match the ceiling or climb performance. Varying accounts

The varied paint schemes of Aggressor aircraft focused attention on their role when the road show visited a unit. George Hall/Check Six

dispute which aircraft had better turning performance, but it was probably so close—with pilot technique, speed, altitude, and model Sabre (solid or slatted wing) all playing a part—that pilot experience would most likely be the deciding factor.

The MiG-15 pilots who fought the Sabres demonstrated a wide range of skill and experience. The North Korean pilots were often very inexperienced, while Soviet pilots were often highly experienced Great Patriotic War (the Soviet term for World War II) veterans, many of them aces. The higher ceiling of the MiG-15 allowed the MiG pilots an altitude sanctuary and the ability to dictate the initial combat, which would invariably be only if they felt they had a position advantage or their opponent was unaware of their presence. The engagements were typically fleeting and intense, many Sabre pilots had to lure the MiG-15 into his altitude and then had only a fleeting chance to engage. The Sabres did well having to develop tactics while engaged in daily battle to try to stop the MiG-15 from breaking through to the bombers and fighter-bombers.

Even as the Korean skies were laced with the contrails of MiGs and Sabres locked in combat, newer aircraft designs were forthcoming that

would lead toward the need for dissimilar aircraft training. The quest and almost obsession with speed led to development of the F-104 Starfighter, F-100 Super Sabre, F4D Skyray, and F8U Crusader. Not all these aircraft gave up maneuverability for speed, but speed became a primary factor. Aircraft began to feature their own radars, and some reasoned that radar directed interceptions and forward firing missiles and rockets would make dogfights a thing of the past.

Theory aside, the post-Korean days were no different regarding impromptu dogfights, especially in the skies over Europe. The various North Atlantic Treaty Organization (NATO) air forces based on the European continent provided ample opportunity for mixing it up. R. J. "Chick" Childerhouse, a Canadian F-86 Sabre pilot related a characteristic impromptu furball over West Germany in his book, *The F-86 Sabre,* published by ARCO in 1965. Airborne on a maintenance test flight, he heard a squadronmate call that he had forty American Sabres "cornered" over Bitburg. His main concern was other Canadian Sabre pilots had also heard the call and were speeding to the engagement and would rob him of the best pickings. Arriving over Bitburg he found the forty Americans all right, but he also dis-

The F-86 Sabre was rushed to Korea to counter the surprise appearance of the MiG-15. Both aircraft were similar in appearance and performance, but each had relative strengths and weaknesses that could be used to advantage. Capt. J. A. Bell

covered that his friend had disengaged, leaving him to face the forty stirred up American Sabres. He narrates:

"The wild blue was never more wild than it was that afternoon over Bitburg. They were everywhere. Blue-banded Sabres, Red-tailed Sabres, yel-

The MiG-21 Fishbed was surrounded by an air of mystery and invincibility until Israeli agents persuaded an Iraqi pilot to defect to Israel with his MiG-21 in 1966. Exploitation and evaluation enabled Israel and the United States to develop tactics to counter this deadly supersonic fighter. via Sam Katz

low-nosed and star-spangled ones. Some had drop tanks, some were clean. They were at ten o'clock, three o'clock, six o'clock. All going for my tail feathers..... The debacle must have lasted twenty minutes. It went on and on.... My tactics were those of desperation too.... Violent scissors, vicious reversals which left me canopy to canopy across twenty yards of space with my pursuer of the moment. Swish! The mid-air collision was averted by someone else, not me.... For the hundredth time, wrench the Sabre high and to the side, fighting for that extra inch of altitude. Two Swords behind, one more sliding in from the near side.... Wallowing Sabre slithers up another fifty feet and flops instead of rolls. High in your canopy, directly overhead in fact, the green earth and a top plan view of a Sabre. Fifty feet below. Closing, as your seven tons of aerodynamic marvel falls.

"What to do? The man you are about to collide with peers straight up at death. His Sabre grows, swells to fill your windscreen....The paint of the blue band which girdles the Sabre below is scabrous. It's the last thing you recollect seeing as the ailerons bite enough to give you a half-twist going straight down."

The Air Force fielded the F-100 followed by a reduced number of F-104s in the late fifties. Both aircraft could achieve supersonic speed in level flight. The F-104 was a contemporary of the MiG-21 and was a virtual rocket ship, little more than a streamlined engine with wings—tiny wings—on it. It was fast, but an F-86 could outturn it. As the F-100 arrived in Europe supplanting the F-86, the pilots thought they had the hottest ship around. They did, in terms of speed, but the Canadian Canadair-built Sabre Mk. 6s were chewing the F-100 up in the swirling dogfights.

As an Air Force F-100C pilot stationed in Germany in 1957, Maj. Everest Riccioni was shocked by the frequent losses to the Canadians and developed the "Double-Attack" tactic that allowed the F-100 to deal with a dissimilar bogey.

In 1978, Maj. Barry Watts, himself a tactician and writer asked if "Riccioni's particular dissimilar bogey problem was anything new in 1957." His own answer is "no" citing the same performance asymmetries that were present in the P-47 and the Fw 190.

The Air Force began forming its first Aggressor squadron in the fall of 1972 by borrowing T-38s from the training command while awaiting procurement of F-5Es. A variety of paint schemes were used along with the original white training command finish. Steve Haskin via Marty Isham

Another Air Force fighter pilot and theoretician, Col. John Boyd, penned the *Aerial Attack Study* and put to paper all the various options in air combat which he deemed finite. He went on to develop a means to quantify and compare fighter performance on paper (after massive computer runs) which became the basis for today's energy maneuverability diagrams. The Air Force conducted Operation Featherduster which pitted the F-86 against the F-104 again finding that absolute speed is not a guarantee of superiority especially against a slower, but better turning opponent unless dissimilar tactics are developed to exploit the speed advantage and avoid the opponent's turning advantage.

Following the Korean conflict, US Air Force doctrine changes resulted in fighter pilots being less prepared for the classic dogfight because of a combi-

The Air Force saw the tremendous results Topgun and dissimilar ACM training had on air-to-air performance over North Vietnam and were quick to beef up the ACM portion of their own Fighter Weapons School at Nellis AFB. Here, a T-38 from the 64th Aggressor Squadron at Nellis wears Soviet-style camouflage. Don Logan via Steve Haskin

nation of training philosophy and the deemphasis of maneuverability in newer aircraft designs. The Air Force began to split its fighter pilots into two separate communities with separate missions and philosophies. It bought the F-94 Starfire, F-89 Scorpion, F-102 Delta Dagger, and F-106 Delta Dart for the interceptor role while the fighter mission went to the F-100 and F-104. The fighters were maneuverable in the traditional sense, but the interceptors were much less maneuverable because they were designed for maximum climb rate and speed, as large a radar as possible, and missile armament. It should surprise no one, then, that the next-generation fighter-interceptor—the F-4 Phantom—was initially more of an interceptor than a classic dogfighter. The new guided air-to-air missiles had spawned the missile-only armed F-4, and the quest for speed was realized by sacrificing the maneuverability and even visibility so crucial to success in air-to-air combat.

Vietnam

Meanwhile, the fledgling NVAF continued to mature under Soviet sponsorship. Their MiG-17s were coupled with an extensive Ground Controlled Intercept (GCI) network and deadly surface-to-air defenses composed of anti-aircraft artillery (AAA) of all calibers and the SA-2 Guideline surface-to-air missile (SAM). North Vietnam was a very inhospitable place for American aircraft. The MiG-17s were turning machines and were armed with cannons for close-in fighting.

The initial bombing of North Vietnam was confined to quick forays across the border and initially included prop-driven South Vietnamese A-1H Skyraiders. The Air Force loaded F-105 Thunderchiefs with bombs and F-100 Super Sabres with Sidewinders as escorts. The Navy was jumped by the fledgling NVAF first. On 3 April 1965 MiG-17s tangled with Navy F-8 Crusaders. Both sides exchanged cannon fire, but neither suffered any losses. The word went out to be on the lookout for MiGs. The next day they appeared again, this time popping out of the haze to execute a hit-and-run attack on F-105s laden with bombs. The escorting F-100s had no time to intervene before a Thud was hit and shot down.

The F-4 Phantom was pressed into service as the fighter, but the community had neglected air-to-air training for years. ACM was forbidden in some units over concerns about losses that traditionally occurred due to aggressive ACM training. As the conflict progressed, the MiGs gained experience and became even more aggressive, forcing strike groups to jettison ordnance in order to fend off their slashing hit-and-run attacks. By the end of 1966, the MiGs were a serious threat, and one that was intensified by the appearance of the MiG-21 in the NVAF. The exchange ratio favored the Air Force, but not by a considerable margin and alarmingly the MiGs forced other losses by working in concert with North Vietnam's integrated air defense system of SAMs and AAA that caused the majority of losses.

Interestingly, the tactics used by the North Vietnamese MiG-21s were similar to those used by Claire Chennault's Flying Tigers over twenty years prior, and not too far from the jungles of Vietnam. As the US Air Force strike formations approached from their bases in Thailand, the GCI network would pick them up and vector the MiG-21s into a high rear position on the formation much as the Flying Tiger P-40s had done to the Japanese. The MiG-21s would make a high-speed diving attack, shooting an Atoll air-to-air missile at any unsuspecting F-4 or F-105 and dive away to safety. Like Chennault, the NVAF chose to engage only on their own terms.

The MiG-21

The MiG-21 became a deadly threat and a mystery much as the Fw

190 had been when it first entered combat. At the same time in the Mideast, the Israeli Defense Force (IDF) was very concerned about the MiG-21 and began an operation to covertly obtain one. On 16 August 1966, an Iraqi Air Force pilot, induced to defect by a beautiful female working for the Israeli intelligence service, flew a MiG-21F to Israel. The MiG-21, dubbed 007, was flown against all Chel Ha'Avir (Israeli Air Force) aircraft to determine relative performance. The results of this intensive dissimilar evaluation were a major input into the outstanding success of the Israeli Air Force during the 1967 war. Prior to the 1967 war, Israeli Mirages encountered Syrian MiG-21s

over the Sea of Galilee on 7 April 1967. The Israeli Mirages shot down seven MiG-21s and lost none of their own. The Mirage pilots weren't the only Israeli pilots to benefit from the detailed knowledge of the MiG-21. In the book *Fighters Over Israel* by Lon Nordeen, a Super Mystere pilot, Yallo Shavit, acknowledges the MiG-21 evaluation as a key to his success in the 1967 war:

"'I had experience fighting the MiG-21 because I was one of those who did the dogfights with the MiG-21 brought by the defecting pilot from Iraq that arrived in 1966. We flew the Super Mystere against the MiG-21, and I knew exactly the position where he sees me and does not see me. I

The T-38 filled an important gap until the higher performing F-5E arrived in 1975. The Aggressor "road show" became a regular feature at Tactical Air Command bases throughout the country, giving a lecture series and flying dissimilar ACM training hops against all the aircrews of the host squadron. Don Logan via Steve Haskin

knew from training that if a MiG-21 and Super Mystere crossed the horizon going down at the same time, it would take the MiG more time to recover from the dive because the Super Mystere was more agile.

"'I came into a barrel roll, and I got him with his nose down. It was at low altitude, about 2,000 feet. He went into a tight turn, and I almost lost him

21

The F-5E was a higher performance air-craft than the T-38, and the F-5E had an air-to-air radar and a weapons system. US Air Force via Marty Isham

because he had a lot of energy, but he made a mistake by changing direction. When he said, "Number one, with all due respect, you are doing OK."

"'I said "Shut up, I'm in the middle of a dogfight." I got the MiG at very low speed—150 knots—300 feet over the hangars. He did a turn, and I fired. He exploded and fell right into

The F-5E turns surprisingly well for a su-personic fighter. In the hands of an Aggres-sor pilot, the Tiger has been known to soundly defeat the much more advanced F-15 Eagle. US Air Force via Marty Isham

the hangars in the middle of the base.'"

The Israelis already had the benefit of a MiG-17 from another defection in 1965 followed by the remarkable incident several months later when Israeli pilots forced seven Syrian MiG-17s to land at an Israeli field after they penetrated Israeli airspace. The pilots and five MiG-17s were returned to Syria. These gave Israel three MiG-17s that were used as a dissimilar training unit to acquaint the Israeli pilots with fighting the nimble MiG-17. Interestingly, these MiG-17s were used against Syria in the 1967 war. During the 1967 War, the Israelis had another stroke of fortune, a flight of six MiG-21s rushing from Algeria to join the fight landed at El Arish in the Sinai Desert, an airfield that had been captured by the Israelis. The Algerian pilots fell victim to Arab propaganda that was boasting of victory over the Israelis. The Israelis kept the MiGs and repatriated the pilots.

The Israelis regarded the MiG-21 to be more valuable than any aircraft in its inventory due to the advantage it gave them over their opponents. Pilots in every conflict, as we have seen, have endeavored to know every detail about the performance of their opponent's aircraft. Having a dissimilar asset allows molding of tactics to emphasize strengths and the knowledge to know in what flight regimes an opponent has an advantage and stay away from them.

The US Air Force and Navy were just as eager to learn about the MiG-17 and MiG-21 fighters they faced in Vietnam. According to the book *Shield of David* by Rubenstein and Goldman, four of the Algerian MiG-21s were shipped to the United States. The 17 February 1969 issue of *Aviation Week & Space Technology* stated that a MiG-21 "was secretly brought to the United States last spring and secretly flight tested by AF pilots to learn firsthand its capabilities and design characteristics." Robert Wilcox revealed in his book *Scream of Eagles* that both the MiG-17 and MiG-21 were kept and test-flown at a secret base in the Nevada desert.

Aggressor lineup at Nellis shows the variety of threat-based paint schemes that *evolved with the Aggressor program. US Air Force via Marty Isham*

To provide dissimilar ACM training for Air Force squadrons in Europe, an additional Aggressor unit was formed at Alconbury, England. Here two pilots from the 527th *Aggressor Squadron engage in time honored tradition of talking with their hands. George Hall/Check Six*

LCdr. Foster "Tooter" Teague and LCdr. Ron "Mugs" McKeown, pilots from Test and Evaluation Squadron Four (VX-4), accumulated hundreds of hours in the MiGs comparing them to American fighters. Teague was particularly impressed with the turning performance of the MiG-17. According to an account in *Scream of Eagles,* during comparative flights, he'd brief his opponent, "'Okay, I'm going to start you at my six and you won't win this fight.... You roll in and call when you're tracking, and that's when the fight starts.... It was a standard joke.'" McKeown likened fighting the MiG-17 in a Phantom to being "a giant with a long rifle trapped in a phone booth with a midget using a knife."

Despite its fabulous tight turning ability, they discovered several significant weaknesses in the MiG-17's performance. The MiG-17 had trouble at higher speeds, locking up by 425 knots and going out of control at 450. It also had a slow roll rate compared to the Phantom. A tactic was devised to exploit this that was basically a variation of the tactics Robert Johnson used in his P-47 dogfight against the Spitfire. If a MiG-17 was chasing a Phantom, the F-4 feinted a roll in one direction and quickly reversed the roll, using its thrust advantage to separate as the MiG-17's pilot tried to follow the rolling maneuver, unable to bring its nose to bear in a firing position. The lessons from this program were disseminated to fleet pilots unable to actually participate in fights against the test MiGs. US pilots now had firsthand knowledge on how to take on the MiGs and exploit their weaknesses. The bombing halt begun in March 1968 allowed the Navy aircrews to take a look at their performance and totally revamp their training.

The NVAF tactics had weaknesses also that were taken advantage of by brilliant leaders such as Col. Robin Olds who was well versed with dissimilar combat tactics from his World War II experience as a P-38 Lightning and P-51 Mustang pilot with twenty-four victories. Olds masterminded Operation Bolo in which his 8th Tactical Fighter Wing lured the MiG-21s of the NVAF into the air on 7 January 1967 by masquerading as an F-105 strike group. Instead of bomb-laden thuds the intercepting NVAF pilots found flight after flight of F-4 Phantoms all loaded for air-to-air combat. Olds' wing shot down seven MiG-21s that day, which was almost half of the NVAF inventory of fifteen MiG-21s. Olds used a vertical vector roll to maneuver to the rear of a tight turning MiG-21, refusing to stay in a horizontal turn with the better turning MiG.

Before the year was out, Olds had returned stateside, and the bombing halt in 1968 caused a hiatus in the aerial contest.

The Navy used this opportunity to initiate a sweeping change in ACM training for F-4 aircrews through the founding of Topgun, which emphasized and was centered on dissimilar air combat training. The Navy's air-to-air success from 1971 to 1973 bore out the Topgun philosophy. Through 1972, the Air Force did not fare as well. In fact, in July, even numbers of Air Force F-4s and MiGs were shot down, while the Navy was well under way to a 12.5:1 exchange ratio. NVAF pilots began to avoid the deadly "gray Phantoms" and sought out the green Air Force Phantoms.

The Air Force wasn't totally blind to the losses, and in 1972 the Fighter Weapons School temporarily suspended its instructor course and devoted its curriculum to Top Off, which included a thirteen-sortie ACM syllabus at Nellis for selected aircrews deploying to Southeast Asia. (Dubbed Top Off, it wasn't hard to guess where the inspiration came from.) The syllabus also included dissimilar training. Robin Olds, with four MiGs to his credit and responsible for much of the Air Force's aerial success in 1966–1968, was also sent in 1972 to Thailand to beef up the sagging air-to-air performance.

Finally, in what must have been a bitter pill to swallow, four Navy F-8 Crusaders and four pilots off USS *Hancock* were sent to Udorn Royal Thai Air Force Base in 1972 to provide dissimilar air combat training to the US Air Force F-4 crews. Cdr. John Nichols was one of the F-8 pilots sent to Udorn. An Air Force general admitted to him, "We used to know this stuff, but we forgot it. We haven't taught it in years. We believed those days were over. I'm afraid we didn't keep the faith."

When Air Force Fighter Weapons School instructors and Top Off students invited Topgun up to Nellis for a visit, the Air Force crews were consistently outflown. In the words of an Air Force Fighter Weapons School instructor at the time, "We were outflown for two reasons: lack of proficiency and outmoded tactics." This was exactly what Commander Nichols was finding

A 527th Aggressor pilot mans up for a dissimilar ACM training mission at RAF Alconbury, England. The squadron transferred seven F-5Es to the Navy's VFA-127 in 1988 as it began transition to the F-16.

Operations with the F-16 were cut short by the decision to close the doors of the 527th, 26th, and 65th Aggressor squadrons. George Hall/Check Six

Air Force squadrons in the Pacific received Aggressor support from the 26th Aggressor Squadron based at Clark AFB, Philippine Islands, and equipped with the T-38 initially. Katsuhiko Tokunaga via Steve Haskin

at Udorn. His impression, as stated in the book he wrote with Barrett Tillman, *On Yankee Station,* "The contest between their F-4s and our F-8s was so uneven that at first we were almost ashamed of the disparity." By the time Nichols left Udorn in September 1972, the Air Force had fully embraced the idea of instituting dedicated dissimilar air combat training and procuring aircraft especially for that purpose.

Aggressor Squadrons

The ultimate solution was to create a dissimilar air combat program with dissimilar aircraft for all Air Force units. The Air Force decided that the F-5E would be the most reasonable aircraft for the role, but they would have to be procured, which would result in an acceptable delay. The T-38 was acceptable as an interim

solution, and they were available in the Training Command. Not having the advantage of ready-made dissimilar air combat aircraft in units that could support the program as did the Navy with their instrument Replacement Air Groups (RAGs), the Air Force decided to create units expressly for the dissimilar role. These units would be called Aggressor squadrons.

A squadron was created at Nellis AFB in October of 1972 specifically for the purpose of providing dissimilar air combat training. The 64th Fighter Weapons Squadron (FWS) was authorized eighteen T-38 aircraft, twenty-two aircrew, and six GCI controllers. Due to the varied locations of Air Force fighter squadrons, the 64th FWS was founded on the idea of taking its aircraft on the road. A typical two-week deployment involved four T-38s with four pilots and two GCI controllers. Usually, forty sorties would be provided to a twenty aircrew unit, giving each crew two dissimilar hops. By June of 1973, the 64th FWS was operational and made its first unit visitation in July.

The T-38s were later replaced by more capable F-5Es, which were intended for the South Vietnamese government but not delivered before the country fell in 1975. This "windfall" allowed the Air Force to equip other Aggressor units.

Aggressor squadrons were formed in England (the 527th FWS at Alconbury) to support Air Force units in Europe, the Philippines (the 26th FWS at Clark AFB) to support units in the Pacific, and a second unit (the 65th FWS) at Nellis to support the stateside demand and for the massive Red Flag exercises flown out of Nellis.

F-5Es were incorporated into the program, and a variety of paint schemes were applied with Soviet-style numbers on the nose. As one of the original Aggressors commented recently, it wasn't hard to focus the attention of the fighter crews on dissimilar training when the Aggressors arrived on base with their threat paint schemes. Ideally each unit would receive a visit from the Aggressors during its six month training cycle and see the Aggressors during Red Flag.

The road show would help build dissimilar skills, and Red Flag served as the test to see how well the unit had learned its craft. The Aggressors became its own community with many pilots staying with the Aggressors moving from unit to unit.

In the late eighties, the Aggressors saw a need to transition to the F-16 in order to more accurately simulate the latest threat aircraft—including the Soviet MiG-29 and Su-27—which were fourth-generation fighters with thrust-to-weight ratios better than 1:1, robust radars with radar-guided missiles, and superb maneuverability. The F-5 fell short in each of these areas, but the F-16 was ideal and already in the Air Force inventory. The 64th FWS was selected to transition to the F-16, but

at the same time, budgetary constraints forced the disbanding of the 65th FWS, reducing the number of assets available for road shows to operational units. By 1989, F-16s began replacing the F-5 at Nellis in the 64th FWS and England in the 527th FWS. As the 527th at Alconbury received F-16s, it gave up its F-5Es which were eagerly accepted by Navy and Marine Adversary squadrons.

Having the same aircraft in tactical squadrons and the Aggressors units caused budget analysts to question why the Aggressors couldn't be done away with and regular tactical F-16 squadrons used to fight F-15 squadrons and vice versa. The argument that the success of dissimilar air combat training was due to the combi-

Another T-38A Aggressor at Clark AFB.
Katsuhiko Tokunaga via Steve Haskin

nation of specially trained instructors as well aircraft did not deter the budget cutters. The budget and the fact that the Aggressors hadn't endeared themselves to all they met resulted in the eventual decision to eliminate the 65th FWS as the transition to the F-16 occurred. The Clark-based 26th FWS briefly operated a few F-16s before another budget cut did away with them as well.

Although budget cuts and the choice of the F-16 as the new Aggressor aircraft hastened the demise of the Aggressors, the squadrons had an image problem as well. The Aggres-

sors were perceived as prima donnas who were more concerned with winning than with training, and their tactics were criticized as being more "anti-Eagle" than true threat simulations. The Aggressor community had been subject to pressure over these concerns and suffered several purges of leadership as a result. Many of the Aggressor "mafia" believed the critical nature of their mission would preserve the units in some form and were shocked when it appeared that the Aggressor mission would never see a

twenty-year anniversary. The England- and Philippines-based units were stood down, and finally, to the surprise of many, the 64th FWS was told to close its doors by October 1990.

Having dedicated units for dissimilar training is a luxury no other air force in the world can afford, but the idea of eliminating the Aggressor training raised the spectre of a return to a lower level of readiness. The Aggressors were an integral part of the modern Air Force whose Red Flag exercises promised it would never enter a war ill-prepared, as it had so many times before.

The plan to use regular Navy units or other tactical squadrons as opponents isn't practical for most Air Force units, but those units located near the four Navy bases having Adversary squadrons are able to take advantage of their services. Langley-

based F-15s use the same TACTS range as the Navy fighters at NAS Oceana and can fight VF-43's F-16s, F-5s, and A-4s, VFC-12's A-4s, or F-14s from any of eleven Tomcat squadrons.

Even so, after the demise of the Air Force Aggressor program in October 1990, Red Flag observers noted a decrease in dissimilar ACM skills on the part of units participating in the exercise because of the lack of Aggressor road-show training. The exercises revealed a decrease in readiness and a clear need for specialized ACM instructors. As a result, the Adversary Tactics Division (ATD) was created under the auspices of Red Flag to provide the specialized training needed. Slowly, the ATD accumulated a few F-16s and painted them in threat paint schemes. The title of aggressor was purposely not used as if in punishment for the transgressions of the past. ATD

This 65th Aggressor F-5E on the ramp at Nellis AFB sports flashy intake covers. K. Minert via Marty Isham

is the only Air Force unit presently conducting dissimilar ACM training.

By 1992, ATD had eight F-16Cs and one F-16D aircraft in service. The small size of ATD does not allow any road shows because Red Flag consumes all their time, but at least some dissimilar training is available.

The hope for increased scope of the Air Force dissimilar program is nurtured by many Air Force fighter pilots, but the budget and defense downsizing doesn't give much cause for opti-

65th Aggressor F-5E down and dirty in the landing pattern. Michael Grove

Two Aggressors lift off at Nellis. Interestingly, the side numbers are different colors indicating a mixed section of 64th and 65th F-5Es. US Air Force via Marty Isham

mism. The need for dissimilar training is clear; the scope and affordability will be the issue in the future. Joint units serving both services is a possibility that has been suggested.

The need for a fourth-generation Aggressor aircraft with greater thrust-to-weight ratio and maneuverability over the F-5E led to the 64th Aggressor Squadrons transition to the F-16. Ironically, the use of the F-16 indirectly resulted in criticisms that the specialized squadrons were no longer necessary because regular F-16 squadrons could serve as dissimilar ACM training assets. This 64th F-16 sports the initial light blue camouflage similar to the MiG-29 Fulcrum's. Marty Isham

The 64th Aggressor flight line in April of 1989 shows variety of paint schemes adopted for the F-16. Marty Isham

Budgetary reality and lack of support for the Air Force Aggressor squadrons brought the program to an end in 1990 when the 64th closed its doors in October. A modest Adversary program was then created under the auspices of Red Flag as the Adversary Tactics Division (ATD), which inherited a few remaining Aggressor F-16s. Eventually, it acquired nine F-16s to fly as bogeys during Red Flag exercises. C. Kaston via Marty Isham

Chapter 3

Navy Dissimilar Air Combat Training and the ACM Renaissance

After World War II, the Navy relegated training in air combat tactics to individual squadrons, resulting in a lack of innovative dissimilar training such as that instituted by LCdr. James Flatley and Lt. Bill Leonard with the captured Zero or LCdr. Jimmy Thach with the restricted-power Wildcats. The advent of the jet age posed its own problems in adapting jets to carrier operations and pilots to jets. When conflict broke out in Korea, the Navy was caught in the middle of the transition to the jet age, resulting in prop-powered aircraft serving alongside their jet brethren.

In the skies over Korea, Navy prop and jet aircraft challenged North Korean prop and jet aircraft. The positioning of and missions flown by Navy and Marine aircraft gave them fewer opportunities for aerial combat than the Air Force experienced. The majority of air combat was fought by Air Force F-86s in their contest with the MiG-15 for mastery of the skies.

Stateside, sister services still delighted in bouncing one another. RAdm. Paul Gillcrist recalls life in a F9F-6 squadron in the late fifties in

The merge—a Topgun F-16 engages an F-14 Tomcat in ACM off the coast of California in 1989. Bob Lawson

The FJ Fury was a naval development of the popular F-86 Sabre and continued the heritage of maneuverable day fighters, while parallel development led to night-fighter or interceptor designs that sacrificed maneuverability for bulky radars and speed. US Navy

The F2H Banshee served alongside the FJ Fury series and was viewed as a night fighter in thought and design. Interestingly, it also was tasked with the seemingly incongruous mission of nuclear attack that involved quite detailed and disparate training from air-to-air interception. US Navy

The F3H Demon was replaced by the F-4 Phantom and left fleet service in September 1964. It was woefully underpowered and produced a generation of pilots and a mentality unprepared to exploit the ACM capabilities of the Phantom. US Navy

The F-4 design packed plenty of performance when it entered service with the fleet at the beginning of the sixties; however, it was viewed as a missile toting interceptor and not a dogfight aircraft because the prevailing doctrine ruled out the possibility of dogfighting in the belief that Sparrow and Sidewinder missiles would eliminate any opponent well before dogfight range was reached. The initial encounters over North Vietnam proved this belief wrong, and the Navy and Air Force found themselves with F-4 communities ill prepared for aerial combat. It was years before tactics based on dissimilar performance were devised to exploit the strengths of the Phantom. US Navy

California when a combat training mission consisted of making a low pass over a nearby F-86D base to draw up the alert pilots for ACM: "I could see the field clearly at fifteen miles, making out the four alert pads, each with a beautiful silver-colored F-86 parked on it, electric starting carts all plugged in, waiting to be scrambled."

His flight of Cougars crossed the field boundary at 330 feet and 530 knots and pulled up into steep climb. "Looking down I could see pilots and ground crews sprinting across the tarmac from the alert shacks to their waiting airplanes," he remembered. "We had just flushed up a covey of quail. Tiny took our division in a gently climbing right-hand circle around the field still at full throttle. The four alert F-86s were now taxiing in a single line at nearly full power down the alert taxiway and onto the runway. The first plane was halfway down the runway and lifting off when Tiny called Mel on the radio.

"'Three, this one rolling in. I've got the first two,' he stated almost casually. The poor bastards never had a chance. I watched Tiny's Cougar bounce the second airplane. It was un-

The first victory over the NVAF was scored by this F-4 aircrew, Cdr. Lou Page (pilot) and LCdr. J. C. Smith (RIO) on 17 June 1965. In an apparent validation of the F-4 interceptor tactics, they were able to visually identify their bogeys as MiG-17s and fire the Sparrow missile head-on. As the war progressed, this success with Sparrows was rarely repeated, and F-4 aircrews found themselves in dogfight situations for which they were ill prepared. US Navy

The aircraft and community best prepared to deal with North Vietnam's nimble and deadly MiGs were the F-8 Crusader and its pilots. The F-8 was the culmination of day-fighter design, and the community never let its ACM skills go slack. By the time of the 1968 bombing halt, the Crusader had the most successful kill ratio of any fighter in use, racking up eighteen victories while losing only three F-8s. Here an F-8E Crusader from VF-211 catapults off the USS Bon Homme Richard (CVA-31) in May 1967, one of the most successful months for the F-8 during the war. US Navy

This overhead view of Navy carrier aircraft with Egyptian aircraft of Soviet and Western origin during a joint exercise in 1985 graphically illustrates the size difference between the F-14 and many of the type of aircraft that it could face in combat. US Navy

merciful. The F-86 was in full burner, tucking away his wheels and flaps and trying to cut across the circle in a rendezvous on his section leader. After a second gunnery run on the leader, Tiny's airplane pulled up in a nearly vertical turn to position himself for a re-attack. All this took place in what seemed like a matter of seconds. As soon as the F-86s picked up some fighting speed, they would turn into their attackers and try to catch us in a slow-speed turning engagement. But we didn't allow ourselves to be drawn into such a fight because the F-86s in full burner could win. Mel kept our energy level high and initiated repeated slashing gun attacks from above the harassed interceptors."

Today, ACM engagements are flown only after briefing all participants on the ground, in most cases, face to face. The rules of engagement that were developed to govern the conduct of ACM training specifically mandate calling off the fight if an unbriefed aircraft enters the fray. The great effort to reduce the horrendous mishap rates of the services led to stricter rules governing free-lance flying. The days of VFR (visual flight rules) flying were shrinking as the pressure to file IFR (instrument flight rules) flight plans became dominant. Due to rising costs and institutionalizing of many of the rules that govern training, air crews can't just "bounce" anyone they encounter.

Fighters and Interceptors

Since the mid-fifties, the fighter component of the Navy carrier air wing had evolved to include a day-fighter and a night-fighter squadron. During World War II, carrier-based night fighters were radar-equipped F6F Hellcats or F4U Corsairs with basically similar performance (less a little drag due to the radome and little weight increase) to their day-fighter brethren. With the introduction of jets, night fighters began to differ in design and performance from day fighters. While the Navy day-fighter series progressed through a variety of models in the fifties from the F9F Panther to the FJ Fury culminating in the F8U Crusader, the night-fighter evolution progressed from the F3D Skyknight to the F2H Banshee, to the F4D Skyray,

and then to the F3H Demon, culminating in the F-4 Phantom. Design of day fighters and night fighters (the term *night* eventually gave way to *all-weather*) had diverged down two separate paths. Furthermore, by dividing the two missions, two communities evolved with different mentalities. Although some "cross-pollination" did occur, by the time the Navy Phantom was placed in the hands of Demon pilots, its potential as an ACM aircraft lay unrealized for several years until a few of the cross-pollinated day-fighter pilots started exploring its potential. This was about the time the Southeast Asia conflict began to erupt. This situation is described by Capt. Dan MacIntyre in the book *Phantom II* by Lou Drendel.

"When I first arrived at the RAG in 1964, I heard many many stories from both the Crusader pilots who had hassled against the Phantom and the Phantom pilots who had tried. According to just about everybody, the Phantom was simply another lump of lead like the Demon, only faster and possessed with a better rate of climb because of the two J-79's it hauled around.'"

At the start of hostilities in Vietnam, the F-8 Crusader was the domi-

nant fighter aircraft in both numbers and in the minds of carrier aviators. The Phantom had entered fleet service in 1961 and was still relatively new to the fleet when the Gulf of Tonkin incident occurred in 1964 and launched the United States into the Vietnam conflict. Eventually the large-deck CVs (aircraft carriers) were to have an F-8 Crusader squadron and an F-4 Phantom squadron. The smaller carriers (27 "Charlies") had two F-8 Squadrons. Later in the conflict most air wings went to two F-4 Squadrons as the F-8 supply dwindled. This occurred over the span of the nine-year conflict in which much was learned about the fighter potential of the Phantom and the crucial role of dissimilar ACM training in developing first-class fighter crews.

Meanwhile, specialized units for air-to-air combat developed. The Fleet Air Gunnery Unit (FAGU) was created at Naval Air Field (NAF) El Centro, California, as a specialized school for training pilots from squadrons to be air-to-air gunnery instructors. They kept air combat skills sharp through the jet age. There was no need for dedicated dissimilar units because the local training areas were rich with potential adversaries. As the rules were

The Navy Fighter Weapons School (Topgun) was established during the Vietnam War to improve the ability of aircrews flying the F-4 against the nimble MiG-17 and MiG-21 that were challenging air superiority. Topgun's austere beginnings forced the initial cadre of instructors to borrow dissimilar aircraft wherever they could. VF-126 was close by and had A-4 Skyhawks used for instrument training. They were used routinely by Topgun as a surrogate for the MiG-17. Randy Cunningham credits a Topgun instructor flying a borrowed VF-126 A-4 with teaching him the moves he needed to best his skilled opponent on 10 May 1972 when he scored three kills in a single mission. Topgun was the first unit in history to be founded on the premise of dissimilar air combat training. Stephen Miller

not as strict as today, massive aerial engagements were commonplace, such as one impromptu fight over San Clemente Island described by Mel Holmes in the Robert Wilcox book *Scream of Eagles,* involving F3H Demons, F-8 Crusaders, F4D Skyrays, and a couple of A-4 Skyhawks. Holmes, in a Skyray, was impressed by his squadronmate Tom Rodgers' performance against the supposedly better performing F-8. Holmes used his low altitude turning advantage

against the F-8 after goading the pilot out of the arena where the F-8 would prevail. While the opportunity for opponents was indeed rich, there was no cadre of instructors or knowledge and, most importantly, no detailed debrief after these engagements.

Another Skyray pilot did get a debrief after being surprised in an encounter with an opponent he should have bested, at least on paper. In 1958, flying an F4D Skyray, Ens. Dan Pederson was lured to the snarled spaghetti of contrails from two aircraft locked in a dogfight. As he closed, he saw a Korean War-vintage F-86 making mincemeat out of an F-8 Crusader, the fleet's latest fighter and, on paper, far superior to the F-86, which was no longer a front-line aircraft and only

A Topgun A-4E Skyhawk on the ramp at NAS Miramar. Stephen Miller

flown by Air National Guard units. Yet, the F-86 was clearly winning. When the F-8 disengaged, Pederson took on the F-86 only to find himself looking back at an F-86 saddled in at his six o'clock. The F-86 pilot knew his own aircraft and enough about the Skyray to avoid the Skyray's strengths and capitalize on his turning performance. Pederson later became Topgun's first CO and was instrumental in establishing formal dissimilar ACM training.

This type of impromptu ACM did not gradually fade from the scene until the late sixties when ACM related mishaps, sonic booms, and widespread flat-hatting brought curtailment upon the "anything goes" atmosphere. Many training activities were forced into specially designated training airspace, much of it over water, away from populated areas. ACM itself wasn't outlawed, it just became more controlled, requiring briefing beforehand and hands off of airliners. As this occurred, many fighter crews were deprived of the chance to fight dissimilar aircraft on a routine basis, although the training airspace did serve as "Indian Country" of sorts.

Phantoms and Crusaders

When the F-4 Phantom entered the fleet in 1961, with it came the notion that missiles would eliminate the dogfight. FAGU was disbanded, and only the F-8 community kept alive the skills of ACM. By 1968 the Phantom was well into replacing the Crusader as the primary air-to-air fighter. That meant F-8 pilots were gradually transitioning into the Phantom and bringing their ACM expertise with them, but the F-4 was an interceptor in both design and philosophy. Its design for Mach-2 performance sacrificed turning performance and visibility, so critical in the dogfight arena. For the first time in fighter history, a fighter carried no gun due to the firm belief that missiles would take care of any opponent before closing to dogfight range. The dwindling community of F-8 pilots referred to themselves as "the last of the gunfighters."

It wasn't long after hostilities broke out in Vietnam that the fallacies of this missile-only intercept approach were revealed. By then, the Air Force

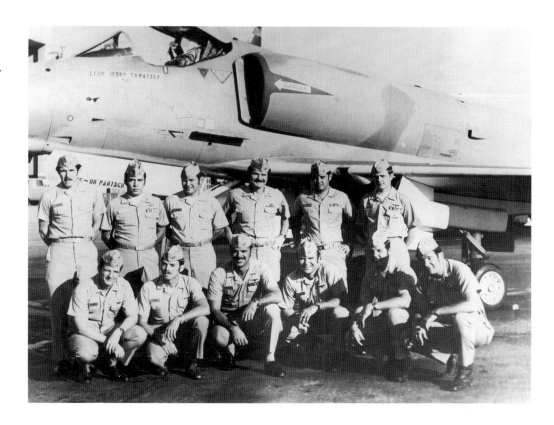

Topgun instructors of the 1973 time frame pose in front of an A-4E "Mongoose." Topgun had on staff several instructors with firsthand experience fighting MiGs: Lt. Randy Cunningham (five kills) is in the bottom row, far right. Lt. (jg) Willie Driscoll (five) is in the top row far left; on Driscoll's right is MiG killer Lt. Winston Copeland (one); and third from the right in the bottom row is Topgun CO, LCdr. Ron McKeown (two). US Navy

The Navy expanded its dissimilar ACM training by using TA-4 Skyhawks already in use by instrument RAGs—VF-126, VA-127, VA-43, and VA-45—that were located at the master jet bases. The existence of the instrument squadrons and their ready transition into the Adversary role was a bonus for the Navy and for the pilots previously relegated to a relatively unrewarding task. There was no resistance to adding the Adversary mission, and it eventually became the squadrons' sole reason for existence. Harry Gann

The Blue Angels were first to operate the powerful A-4F Super Fox derived from the up-rated J52-408 engine installed in the Kuwaiti A-4KU Skyhawks. Eventually this hottest performing A-4 began to filter into the Adversary program. At low fuel weights, the Super Fox had better than a 1:1 thrust-to-weight ratio, making it a formidable Adversary. The A-4F became available for Adversary service as the A-7 Corsair progressively replaced the A-4 in fleet service. US Navy by Hiroshi Seo

had adopted the F-4 as well and was in a similar predicament, but the stop-and-go nature of the air war over North Vietnam masked many problems. The air-to-air contest over North Vietnam was not of the same intensity as Korea or World War II. It was cyclic in nature due to weather and the periodic stand downs of the fledgling NVAF. Some Navy squadrons never even saw MiGs, so it was difficult to assess the performance of aircrews and identify problems. It was almost a year after the Gulf of Tonkin incident that MiG-17s challenged US aircraft. In fact after two Air Force F-105s were lost to MiG-17s on 4 April 1965, it was F-4 Phantoms that first avenged the loss. Navy F-4B's downed two MiG-17s in June followed by Air Force F-4Cs downing another pair of MiG-17s in

July resulting in early confidence in the Phantom and its tactics.

However, by the time of the bombing halt in 1968, the Crusader had showed its mettle downing eighteen MiGs in twenty-five engagements, a kill-per-engagement ratio of 0.72. During the same period of time Navy Phantoms downed twelve MiGs in thirty-nine encounters (0.30). Cdr. John Nichols, an F-8 pilot credited with one of the MiGs, attributes the difference to training. He also points out that "they were allowed to risk airplanes while perfecting their skills," and that the loss of an F-8 during ACM training was "the price one paid for proficiency in aerial combat." The Crusader community's emphasis on ACM prowess was borne out in their overall exchange ratio of 6.3:1 (nineteen victories, three losses) against the North Vietnamese MiGs. This was better than any other aircraft in any service.

The Ault Report and Topgun

At the time of the bombing halt, the Naval Air Systems Command took several initiatives to improve the air-combat performance of Navy aircrews. One of these was to empower Capt. Frank Ault, returning CO of the USS

Coral Sea to conduct a no-holds-barred top-to-bottom study of the problem. The resultant report, now often referred to as the Ault Report, looked at everything from missile-handling procedures to the quality of training afforded the Phantom crews. A crucial observation was the vast difference in performance between the Phantom and MiG-17. From the Israeli Air Force experience with the MiGs, it was obvious that dissimilar ACM training was the key to defeating the MiGs. The overall problem was the lack of ACM focus in F-4 training, but as the Ault Report revealed, the combined effect of many problems such as poor missile-handling procedures, maintenance, and missile performance were exacerbating the F-4 community's problems in air-to-air combat.

The most important result of the Ault Report was the formal endorsement of the Navy Fighter Weapons School, which had been formed about the same time the report was being written as an offshoot of the West Coast F-4 RAG, VF-121, at NAS Miramar. The CO of VF-121 installed LCdr. Dan Pederson as the head of a new department charged with developing a graduate-level ACM tactics syllabus for training F-4 aircrews. Pederson and his fellow instructors purloined a trailer (among other things) from Miramar's base ops and began building an independent school within VF-121 by late 1968. The result was a renaissance in the approach to teaching ACM, especially in the F-4 community. The department became known as Topgun and eventually acquired its own aircraft and became an independent command in 1972.

The first class, which included aircrews from VF-142 and VF-143, convened on 3 March 1969 and lasted an intense four weeks. It included a mix of academics and flying. A key ingredient was use of dissimilar ACM training to develop, validate, and teach tactics. Topgun graduated six classes from its four-week course in 1969, seven classes in 1970, and eight in 1971, each with six to eight crews. The Topgun graduates were expected to become ACM instructors for their squadrons. The ACM potential of the Phantom was being explored more than ever.

The Navy decided to use the A-4 Skyhawk, which was similar in size and performance to the MiG-17, as its first Adversary aircraft. It was available in ample numbers as it was still in service in both training and fleet squadrons. Topgun initially borrowed A-4s from VF-126, an instrument training RAG co-located at Miramar. When Topgun became an independent command, it acquired several Skyhawks of its own. F-8s were locally available at Miramar to simulate MiG-21s, and by 1970 it also had a formal agreement with the Air Force Air Defense Command to fight its F-106 Delta Darts.

By the time the air war over North Vietnam heated up again in January 1972, Topgun was well established and acknowledged to be the leader in F-4 tactical thought. It was a Topgun graduate, Lt. Randy "Duke" Cunningham, who scored the first victory. Four months later, he scored four more times, and became the first US ace of the conflict. His last engagement was a protracted duel with a pilot who was thought to be one of North Vietnam's leading aces. During this closely fought match, Cunningham recalled lessons learned during a Topgun dissimilar hop against an A-4. Locked in a vertical rolling scissors with the MiG-17, he remembered "Dave Frost, a Topgun instructor, had taught [him] how to disengage in this situation." In fact one of the thoughts that came to

his mind was, "I've been here before!" Cunningham had over 150 dissimilar ACM training hops prior to combat. That simply would not have happened prior to Topgun.

VF-96, Cunningham's squadron, had five Topgun trained crews on board prior to deploying to Southeast Asia in 1971. According to Capt. Dwight Timm, executive officer at the time, "We really used their Topgun experience to teach the entire squadron the art of dogfighting." It apparently worked as VF-96 came away with a record eight victories.

Randy Cunningham went on to later instruct at Topgun and eventually command an Adversary squadron, VF-126. The phrase "You fight the way you train" has been immortalized by Cunningham.

Topgun took the lead in turning the F-4 community into a fearsome air-combat force. In 1972, Navy Phantoms scored twenty-four times in twenty-three engagements coming away with a 12:1 loss ratio. During the same time period the Air Force was scoring against the same MiGs as well, but suffered some setbacks. In June, seven Air Force aircraft were lost to MiGs while only two were shot down in return. In July, it was six each. While the Navy was finally vindicating their pre-Topgun performance, the Air Force kill-to-loss ratio was lower in 1972 than it had been in 1968. Reportedly, the North Viet-

Two A-4F Skyhawks display their Adversary colors in 1983 during a detachment to NAS Fallon. Michael Grove

namese pilots were told to stay away from the gray (Navy) Phantoms and to go after the green (Air Force) Phantoms.

By the time American forces left the war zone, the Navy had scored twenty-five times after Topgun and suffered only two losses. The Air Force kill-to-loss ratio remained at around 2:1. The Navy investment in dissimilar ACM training and Topgun had proved itself beyond a doubt.

After the cessation of hostilities, Topgun continued to grow, adding several aircrew to the staff fresh from victories over the North Vietnamese including Cunningham and his radar intercept officer (RIO), Lt. (jg) Willie Driscoll, Lt. Winston "Mad Dog" Copeland (one victory), and LCdr. Ron "Mugs" McKeown (two victories) who reported as the new CO. His RIO, Lt. Jack Ensch (two victories) reported after repatriation from his POW status.

Adversary Aircraft

McKeown led the charge on acquiring aircraft for the school to call their own. Initially, Topgun had borrowed Skyhawks from VF-126. It wasn't difficult to convince VF-126 to fly ACM along with their instrument-

In 1985, VF-43 introduced the Israeli F-21A Kfir into the Adversary community, which allowed large-scale supersonic formations for the first time. Here a VF-101 Tomcat returns to NAS Oceana after a dissimilar ACM training mission. Dana Potts

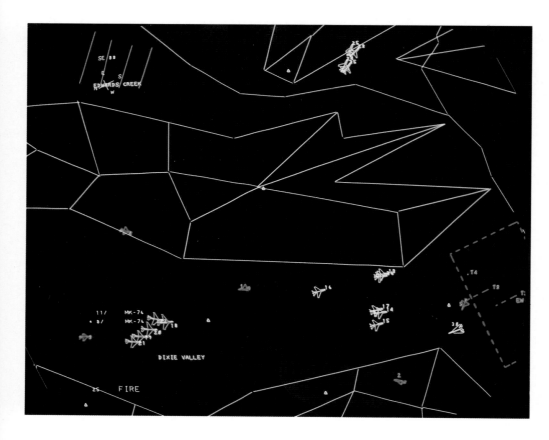

Designed by the Cubic Corp. of San Diego, California, the TACTS system at NAS Fallon can track up to thirty-six aircraft, display their positions in real time, simulate air-to-air and surface-to-air missile launches, record it all, and then play it back later so the pilots can see and learn from any mistakes. This display shows a "God's Eye" view of a strike group proceeding over the Fallon range to a target defended by A-4 Adversaries. The geometric lines represent mountains. Cubic Corp.

qualification duties, and the TA-4's slow speed characteristics were suitable to simulate the MiG-17 and the MiG-21 (at slower speeds). The maneuverability of the Skyhawk was a counter to the high-speed performance of the F-4, which made it the ideal Adversary aircraft. Topgun acquired some single-seat A-4E Skyhawks that were even better performing than the TA-4J and stripped them down, disabled the wing slats, and painted them in representative threat paint schemes.

McKeown wanted a supersonic bogey, as well, to simulate the MiG-21. The F-8 was rapidly leaving the inventory, and although the Aerospace Defense Command was willing to fly ACM with their F-106s, Topgun needed an aircraft flown by a Topgun instructor. Finally, three early-model Air Force T-38 Talons were located. They needed work, but the Air Force was willing to give them to the Navy as it wasn't worth the trouble to bring them up to definitive T-38 standard, and they were hard to support. Topgun eagerly brought them down to Miramar and used every connection it had in order to make them ready for ACM training. Even a few flight jackets reportedly changed hands to get the requisite parts. Topgun now had supersonic Adversaries.

In 1975, a number of brand-new F-5E Tigers originally intended for South Vietnam became available. The Navy asked for nine, six of which went to Topgun. The F-5E and A-4E became the mainstay of Topgun until the arrival of the F-16N in 1987. The instrument RAG aircraft began sporting camouflage paint schemes like those initiated at Topgun for its A-4s.

The advent of fourth-generation fighters such as the F/A-18, F-16, MiG-29, and others, called for a new Adversary aircraft with the performance equal to that of the MiG-29. The need for an improved Adversary was exacerbated by the growing number of F/A-18s replacing the A-7, in effect doubling the need for Adversary services. While the Navy was selecting its new Adversary aircraft, Israel offered Kfir fighters (modified, Israeli-built Mirages) on a no-cost lease basis (excluding maintenance costs). Eventually, the Israeli offer was accepted

for a three-year lease on twelve aircraft.

VF-43 was selected to operate the Kfir (designated F-21A), and had the first three in service by April of 1985. VF-43 soon had twelve Kfirs in service, allowing the largest formation of supersonic Adversaries ever assembled in the Navy.

An additional offer for twelve more F-21 Kfirs was accepted, and in 1987, they equipped the first dedicated Marine Adversary squadron, VMFT-401, based at Marine Corps Air Station (MCAS) Yuma, Arizona. This gave the Marines more flexibility in providing Adversary services to their fighter (VMF) and attack (VMA) squadrons. The Yuma location is ideal for support of Marine Aviation Weapons and Tactics Squadron One (MAWTS-1) and its twice annual all-arms exercises.

Pilots praised the Kfir, and the aircraft gave valuable service, but in early 1988 the Navy decided not to renew the Kfir lease because of the high cost of the maintenance support contract. The Kfirs were ferried to

NAS Norfolk in preparation for return to Israel. Plans to equip VF-43 with the F-16N after the departure of the Kfirs were initially delayed until the support contract could be modified. (The civilian maintenance support contract did not allow transfer of F-16s from Key West.)

The Navy decided to buy twenty-six F-16N aircraft for its Adversary squadrons. Basically a stripped down F-16C, with no cannon or defensive electronics, the F-16N became the ultimate Adversary. It can simulate a wide range of threats and provides a worthy Adversary for both the F/A-18 and the newly arrived F-14A (Plus). The first two F-16Ns arrived at Topgun in late April 1987, and two were received each month until all twenty-six were in service with Topgun, VF-126, and VF-45.

The Navy planned to keep its A-4s, but the F-5 would slowly be replaced because of wing fatigue. VFA-127 received the available F-5Es and moved from NAS Lemoore, California, to NAS Fallon, Nevada.

The need for a fourth-generation Adversary led to procurement of twenty-six F-16Ns, which began arriving at Topgun in April 1987 at the rate of two per month. Here the first two F-16s taxi into the Topgun line on 17 June 1987. LCdr. Dave Baranek

In late 1989, the Marine Kfirs were returned to Israel and the squadron began operating the F-5E which was available from Air Force Aggressor squadrons converting to the F-16. During 1989, VF-45 transferred six F-16Ns to VF-43, both squadrons received F-5Es.

In 1991, A-4M Skyhawks became available to replace the tired A-4E Skyhawks, and Topgun received four F-14A Tomcats of its own for use as Adversaries. One Tomcat was painted in Iranian markings and another as an Su-27 Flanker.

Adversary Squadrons

The idea of dedicated Adversary pilots and aircraft to support the F-4 RAGs was popular, and the Navy fighter community found an un-

The transition of Air Force Aggressors to the F-16 and disestablishment of the 65th Aggressor Squadron resulted in a surplus of F-5E Tigers that the Navy took advantage of by equipping VFA-127 and VMFT-401 with the F-5. Seven F-5Es were ferried from England's 527th Aggressor Squadron by VFA-127 pilots, several of which are shown here after their arrival and before VFA-127 markings had been applied. US Navy

Former Marine A-4Ms were used to replace aging A-4Es and A-4Fs in service with VF-126 and Topgun. The "Mike" has the same engine as the Super Fox but is slightly heavier. Despite its advanced age, the A-4 will continue to be a worthy Adversary up to its retirement from the Adversary community in 1994. Dave Parsons

planned asset in the form of instrument RAGs. Instrument RAGs—large training squadrons—were created to transition pilots to navigation and instrument flying in jets. The instrument RAGs took pilots fresh out of flight school and gave them a series of hops flying "under the hood" while flying the jetways and instrument approaches. They also trained pilots transitioning from props to jets and pilots returning from desk jobs. Initially, the instrument RAGs were equipped with a variety of aircraft, principally the F9F-8T Cougar. Attack Squadron Forty-three (VA-43), based at NAS Oceana, also flew the Cougar as an instrument training aircraft. Eventually, the TA-4 Skyhawk became the standard mount of these squadrons when it became available in the late sixties.

It wasn't long before other instrument RAGs also began flying ACM missions as well. VF-126 at NAS Miramar; VA-45 (later VF-45) at NAS Oceana and Key West; and VA-127 (later VFA-127) at NAS Lemoore (now at NAS Fallon) all became full-time Adversary squadrons and eventually shucked the instrument-training mission. Reserve A-4 composite (VFC) squadrons also added Adversary work to their repertoire.

VF-101's Key West detachment acquired three A-4Es of their own specifically for dissimilar ACM training.

When Topgun received F-5Es in 1975, two T-38s were transferred to VF-43 which was increasing its percentage of Adversary missions. It also acquired single-seat A-4s that were becoming available due to the fleet and reserve transition from the A-4 to the A-7. Had the instrument RAGs not existed, it is entirely possible that the Adversary program would have never grown the way it has.

Meanwhile, in the late seventies, the fleet composite squadrons—VC-1, VC-5, VC-8, and VC-10—were authorized to conduct dissimilar ACM training, and they began sending pilots to Topgun to qualify as Adversary pilots. VC-5 became the primary Adversary for the forward-deployed USS *Midway* (Philippines) and provided regular bogey services for the massive joint Cope Thunder exercises held in the Western Pacific. The other VC squadrons were located in fleet training areas frequented by aircraft carriers as well as shore-based squadrons. VC-8 is a regular Adversary for East Coast air wings deploying to NAS Roosevelt Roads, Puerto Rico. VC-1 fought Marine F-4s and later F/A-18s from MCAS Kaneohe Bay, Hawaii, before it gave up its A-4s in 1991. VC-10 maintained A-4s for fleet support and defense of Guantanamo Bay.

The Marine Corps headquarters and maintenance squadrons (H&MS), later changed to Marine aviation logis-

VFC-13 operates the A-4F Super Fox in addition to the TA-4J out of NAS Miramar and will transition to the F/A-18A Hornet in 1994. Bob Lawson

tics squadrons (MALS), also took on Adversary work with their A-4s. The Marines used their TA-4Js that were in H&MS units for years as adversaries. MALS-31 was flying dissimilar ACM training for Marine Aircraft Group Thirty-one (MAG-31) as late as 1990, flying their six TA-4Js an average of 2,500 hours a year. MALS-24 operated TA-4Js out of MCAS Kaneohe Bay, Hawaii, flying an average of 300 dissimilar ACM training sorties annually.

VA-45 and VA-127 supported the A-7 attack community as they established a need for defensive ACM training as part of their RAG syllabus.

Today, Adversary services are available from VF-43 and VFC-12 at NAS Oceana, VF-126 and VFC-13 at NAS Miramar, VF-45 at NAS Key West, and VFA-127 at NAS Fallon. On 1 October 1993, VF-43 and VF-126 will stand begin to down, turning over their responsibilities to VFC-12 and VFC-13.

FFARP

In 1978, VF-43 introduced dissimilar ACM training into RAG training and developed a formal dissimilar

Until recently, VC-1 operated Skyhawks out of NAS Barber's Point, Hawaii, in an Adversary role supporting Pacific Fleet carriers, Marine Hornets at MCAS Kaneohe Bay, and Air Force F-15s at Hickam AFB. US Navy

ACM training syllabus for East Coast fighter squadrons. The syllabus included an intensive series of missions and lectures over a three-week period, starting with one-versus-one and working up to four-versus-many. This training was dubbed the Fleet Fighter ACM Readiness Program. FFARP was

VC-5 operated Skyhawks out of Cubi Point, Philippines Islands, until the closure of the base. The squadron provided Adversary services to Carrier Air Wing Five aboard forward deployed USS Midway. Rick Burgess

Reserves at NAS Dallas had the support of Operations Maintenance Division TA-4Js that were assigned to the station directly. Three A-4Ms were added in 1987 to support the two Naval Reserve Tomcat squadrons and the Marine Reserve F/A-18 Hornet squadron. Rick Burgess

The Marines got their first dedicated Adversary squadron in 1987 when VMFT-401 was formed at MCAS Yuma, Arizona, and equipped with thirteen Israeli F-21A Kfirs. Dave Parsons

VMFT-401 added the F-5E to its inventory in 1989 which replaced the Kfir when they were returned to Israel later that year. Bob Lawson

an instant hit with the fleet. It guaranteed dissimilar ACM training for every squadron during each turnaround period between cruises.

In 1980, VF-126 developed a similar program called TAP (Turnaround ACM Program) for the West Coast squadrons. TAP was later standardized with the East Coast FFARP in 1983. The introduction of FFARP marked the switch to dissimilar ACM training as a primary mission for the instrument RAGs. Today, simulators allow instrument qualification and re-

Topgun had maintained a long-standing requirement to operate its own F-14 Tomcats to simulate the MiG-31 and keep staff proficient in the Tomcat. Four Tomcats were assigned in 1991 with one painted in Iranian markings, another as a Su-27 Flanker, and the remaining two in low visibility gray. A ground mishap claimed one Tomcat and the "Flanker" was transferred back to squadron service with VF-51 in 1992. Dave Parsons

qualification to be conducted without a flight.

Once during the turnaround training period between cruises, the entire squadron participates in a FFARP. Since the early eighties, both coasts have used a thirteen-sortie FFARP syllabus. Academics precede a gradual work-up to multi-bogey hops, all on the TACTS range, and all flown against Topgun-trained Adversary pilots in dissimilar aircraft. The entire process is continually changing to give realistic training for the latest threats and is ideal for validation of tactics. Jimmy Thach would be pleased.

To accurately represent newer threat aircraft, new aircraft types have been introduced into the Adversary role. Throughout the seventies the A-4 and T-38 bore the brunt of Adversary work, being joined by the F-5E. Thanks to the Blue Angels, a special A-4 Super Fox—an A-4F equipped with the J52-P408 engine that gave it a better than 1:1 thrust ratio at lower fuel weights—also become available in the later seventies. It was the favorite mount of many Adversary pilots, and all the squadrons clamored to get their hands on one. VF-43 received a Super Fox as a back-up for the Blue Angels and found it to be awesome in the Adversary role. VF-101 students and fleet aircrews quickly learned the side number of the Super Fox; it wasn't their favorite aircraft to go one-on-one with. Topgun also received two-place F-5Fs and relinquished their T-38s in the late seventies. VF-43 held on to their T-38 until the early eighties.

SFARP

The arrival of the F/A-18 Hornet into the fleet in 1984 created a substantial increase in need for dissimilar ACM training. VF-45 and VFA-127 were situated to support the respective F/A-18 RAGs and began instituting dissimilar ACM training for the Hornet community, which was mainly composed of A-7 squadrons transitioning to the F/A-18. The transitioning pilots were well versed in dropping bombs but had little experience in air-to-air combat.

VF-45 was tasked with developing a version of the F-14 FFARP for Hornet squadrons. The Hornet version of FFARP was dubbed Strike Fighter

ACM Readiness Program and is closely related to FFARP, except the advance hops include self-escort missions. SFARP was popular with the fledgling Hornet community, but it was found that transition squadrons had difficulty with the complicated multi-bogey hops. Consequently, a mini-SFARP was developed as a stepping stone for the Hornet squadrons and conducted four to six months prior to the entire SFARP.

Downsizing the Adversaries

The next significant change in the Adversary program was no longer growth. The downsizing of the US defense budget forced a hard look at the Adversary program. VC-1 and VC-5 had been shut down in September 1992. VFA-127 was the first unit to bid farewell to the A-4 when it received F/A-18 Hornets in 1992, operating them alongside the F-5E. The decision was made to stand down both VF-43 and VF-126 in September 1993 and

The latest Adversary aircraft is the F/A-18A Hornet, which entered service with VFA-127 in 1992. McDonnell Douglas via Lon Nordeen

rely on Fighter Composite Squadrons Twelve and Thirteen (VFC-12 and VFC-13) for fleet Adversary support, including FFARP. Both squadrons will transition to the F/A-18 Hornet in late 1993 and retire their A-4s, a decision based on the increased cost of supporting several types of a thirty-year-old aircraft.

Though the Air Force's Aggressors are gone, it's too soon to sound the death knell for the Navy's Adversaries. Adversary squadrons have proven their worth and have deep support of the fleet squadrons which constantly rely on their support. The varied colors of the Adversary are likely to grace the skies over naval bases as long as there are fighters.

WA
ATD

AF860271

Chapter 4

The US Air Force Adversary Tactics Division

When the 64th FWS stood down on 1 October 1990, the 4440th Tactical Fighter Training Group (TFTG), which hosts the Red Flag exercises, was left with no Aggressor assets except for visiting units not schooled as adversaries. Red Flag serves as the ultimate combat training exercise for the Air Combat Command (formerly Tactical Air Command). The Red Forces must be able to simulate the most stressing threat that Air Force units could possibly face in actual combat. Recognizing the need for a Red Force counterair component to support Red Flag, the Air Force planned to allow six F-16s to be retained under the auspices of Red Flag. After the 64th stood down, the 4440th TFTG established the Adversary Tactics Division (ATD) to maintain the specialized expertise of the Aggressors on a smaller scale. Headed by a lieutenant colonel and staffed with thirteen pilots, ATD is not a squadron, but

the division CO is equivalent to a squadron CO. The ATD's complement of aircraft has since been expanded to eight F-16Cs and one F-16D.

The Aggressors had filled an important role in obtaining from the intelligence community the latest information on potential enemy aircraft

The Adversary Tactics Division (ATD) was created as a division under Red Flag to provide dissimilar adversaries for Red Flag and its associated exercises at Nellis. ATD took over F-16Cs used by the 64th Aggressor Squadron when it closed its doors in October 1990. B. Niedermeier via Marty Isham

ATD did not initially assume all the 64th's aircraft, some of which were transferred to the USAF Fighter Weapons School. By

1992 when this photo was taken, ATD had built up to nine F-16s (eight C models and one D). Dave Parsons

ATD retained the paint schemes used by the 64th Aggressors. Unlike the Aggressors, ATD does not have the assets to conduct road shows and supports only activities at Nellis. B. Niedermeier via Marty Isham

and tactics and incorporating it into their academic portion of their road-show training conducted at various fighter bases. ATD is unable to maintain the road-show tradition because of its limited resources, but continues to produce detailed threat briefings to present to aircrews as they participate in Red Flag.

The Red Force bandits have the advantage of flying over the same real estate continuously, which gives them the tremendous home-field advantage over the visiting Blue Forces. This enhances their simulation of the threat, reflecting the fact that in most potential conflicts, Air Force pilots would be flying over unfamiliar territory defended by air forces very familiar with their home turf and supported by extensive GCI, AAA, and SAM defenses.

In comparison to the four-squadron-strong Aggressor community of the seventies and eighties, ATD is a very modest undertaking. As the CO of Red Flag said recently, "My hope is that one day a four-star general will walk through here and see the role our Adversary Tactics guys play, and say, 'Damn! We lost the bubble, We need more of this capability.' Because it's true. For all their ups and downs, the Aggressors were dearly needed."

ATD retains the Soviet-style red numerals used by the 64th Aggressor Squadron and the 57th Fighter Weapons Wing insignia. Dave Parsons

ATD's two-seat F-16D allows a guest on ACM hops. Marty Isham

Chapter 5

The Navy Fighter Weapons School (Topgun)

The Navy Fighter Weapons School, commonly known as Topgun, is located at NAS Miramar, California. Its origin stemmed from poor performance of the F-4 Phantom against the fledgling NVAF during 1965–1968. Several initiatives were begun to improve the performance of Navy aircrews in the air combat arena. One of these was to empower Capt. Frank Ault, returning CO of the USS Coral Sea to conduct a no-holds-barred top-to-bottom study of the problem. Meanwhile, the CO of VF-121, the West Coast F-4 Phantom RAG installed LCdr. Dan Pederson as the head of a new department of VF-121 charged to develop a graduate-level tactics syllabus for training F-4 aircrews. Pederson began building his school within VF-121 by late 1968. The first class, which included aircrews from VF-142 and VF-143, convened on 3 March 1969 and lasted four weeks. It included a mix of academics and flying. A

Topgun received the first F-16N on 17 June 87. The F-16N heralded a new dimension in Adversary capability with its phenomenal thrust to weight, maneuverability, and digital radar, making it surrogate for the so-called fourth-generation series of threat fighters such as the MiG-29. Here a Topgun F-16N flies vertically with a VF-213 Tomcat. Bob Lawson

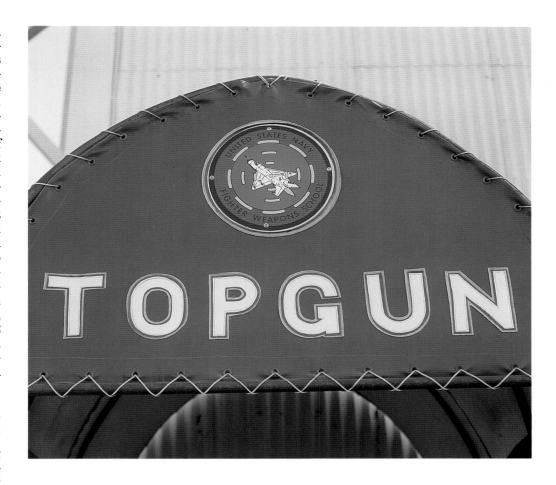

The awning over the entrance to the Navy Fighter Weapons School hangar proclaims the name by which it is more universally known—Topgun. Students and staff alike use Topgun rather than the formal name. Dave Parsons

When Topgun acquired its own aircraft, the A-4E Skyhawk was readily available due to transition of fleet A-4 squadrons to the A-7 and reserves to the A-4F. The single-seat Skyhawk was a step up from the TA-4Js borrowed from VF-126 and a suitable surrogate for the MiG-17. The avionics hump was later removed to lesson the weight and reduce drag, making the Skyhawk a true hot rod. The slats have been bolted up to reduce drag as well. Topgun's staff has Marine members and marks some of its aircraft with Marine markings. Stephen Miller via Rick Burgess

key ingredient was use of dissimilar ACM training to develop, validate, and teach tactics. Skyhawks were borrowed from VF-126 to simulate the MiG-17. F-8 Crusaders and F-106 Delta Darts were used to emulate the MiG-21. The result was a renaissance in ACM training. The department became known as Topgun, eventually acquired its own aircraft, and became an independent command in 1972.

By the time the air war over North Vietnam heated up again in 1972, Topgun was well established and acknowledged to be the leader in F-4 tactical thought and spurred the expansion of officially sanctioned dissimilar ACM training to the instrument RAGs. Topgun also became the driver in standardizing qualifications and rules of engagement.

Topgun initially acquired several A-4E Skyhawks and later resurrected a couple of cast-off T-38 Talons from the Air Force through sheer horse-trading on the part of LCdr. "Mugs" McKeown who took over the school after returning from downing two MiG-17s in 1972. In 1975, a number of brand-new F-5E Tigers originally intended for South Vietnam became available. Topgun got six.

The F-5E and A-4E became the mainstay of Topgun until the arrival of the F-16N in 1987. Topgun gave up its F-5Es and flew the F-16N alongside its A-4E and A-4F Skyhawks. After the arrival of the F/A-18 in 1984

Topgun expanded its syllabus to support Hornet, Tomcat, and Adversary squadrons. In 1991, A-4M Skyhawks became available to replace the Topgun's older Skyhawks, and Topgun received four F-14A Tomcats of its own for use as Adversaries. One Tomcat was painted in Iranian markings and another as an Su-27 Flanker.

Today, Topgun retains its central role in coordinating and standardizing all Adversary training and doctrine for the Navy and Marine Corps. Up to sixty Adversary pilots have been trained per year in the three-week Adversary course. This is in addition to the six-week Power Projection course that is the primary focus of the school. The Power Projection course trains squadron aircrews to return to their squadron and instruct. Topgun has grown incredibly since its inception and sits at the pinnacle of fighter aviation. Topgun sends out periodic road shows to visit squadrons and conduct Fleet Air Superiority Training (FAST).

To simulate the performance of the MiG-21, Topgun found some early production T-38s that were unattractive to the Air Force due to their noncompatibility with the definitive production standard and therefore harder to maintain. A series of trips were made by the staff to get necessary support to make them operational. Note two MiG kill symbols under LCdr. Jack Ensch's name on the rear cockpit. Stephen Miller via Rick Burgess

For most of Topgun's existence, the combination of the F-5E, A-4E, and A-4F has served the school's mission well as the mainstay from 1975 through 1987. A variety of paint schemes such as shown here have graced the aircraft through the years. LCdr. Dave Baranek

The F-5F was the last of the F-5 Tiger II to be received by Topgun, although a two-seater, it retains full systems of the F-5 minus one 20mm cannon. LCdr. Dave Baranek

To its credit, it has played a significant role in avoiding the intra-service rivalries that brought on the demise of the Air Force Aggressors by standardizing Adversary doctrine and fighting to keep egos in check in a very ego-oriented business. Its recent change in status to an Echelon II command, reporting directly to the Pentagon, reflects the vital role Topgun continues to play.

Topgun painted several F-5Es with fictitious markings for flight scenes filmed for the movie Top Gun. *(Note: the school uses Topgun as one word, but the movie uses it as two.)* Michael Grove

The F-16N has proven to be a superlative Adversary capable of simulating a wide range of the latest threat aircraft. The only drawbacks have been some structural problems (cracks in the wing carry-through), which led to curtailment of use on the high-time Topgun F-16s until a fix could be devised and implemented. This F-16 wears a pattern similar to the Swedish Viggen, but not because Sweden is viewed as a potential Adversary, but rather to evaluate the pattern's effectiveness. Note the F-16 in right background undergoing a paint job. Dave Parsons

Topgun has long wanted its own Tomcats for use as Adversaries. In 1991, the school finally acquired four Tomcats that allow simulation of the MiG-31 and keep staff current in the F-14. This Tomcat wears the markings of the Su-27 Flanker, which proved so realistic at a glance that a Topgun stopover visit to an Air Force base resulted in base personnel believing a Flanker had actually dropped into their midst. The crew was greeted by a contingent of security personnel, who were understandably a little excited until the aircrew proved they were from Topgun in an Adversary Tomcat. Rick Burgess

Chapter 6

VF-43 Challengers

VF-43 has been the longest term resident of NAS Oceana, having taken up residence in the earliest days as VF-21.

The squadron was created as VF-74A as part of the original air group assigned to USS *Midway* (CVB-41) in May of 1945. In August, the designation was changed to VF-74, followed by a change to VF-1B in November of 1946. The squadron took its F4U-4 Corsairs aboard USS *Midway* in October of 1947 for the carrier's maiden cruise.

The squadron became VF-21 in September of 1948 and transitioned to F9F-2 Panthers in the spring of 1950. The F9F-7 Cougar arrived in July of 1953, and the squadron made a smooth transition to the swept-wing

The squadron gave up its F-5Es in 1985 and transitioned to the Israeli Kfir, which was designated F-21A in service. The Kfir gave the squadron a significant boost in numbers of supersonic bogeys it could put in the air. The Kfir was operated until 1988 when support-cost disputes and need for a fourth-generation Adversary resulted in the transition to the F-16N. Here two Kfirs fly over the Nevada countryside equipped with TACTS pods for use on NAS Fallon's vast TACTS range in support of a carrier air wing's weapons deployment to Fallon. LCdr. Ken Neubauer

fighter, as evidenced by the winning of the Battle E for that year. In 1955, the Cougar gave way to the FJ-3 Fury, and the squadron was the first to land aboard the newly commissioned USS *Forrestal* (CV-59) in 1956.

During this time, the squadron insignia featured a mailed fist smashing the word Mach on a background of blue and red stripes. At the time, the squadron referred to themselves as the Mach-busters or Mach-knockers. In May of 1957, the squadron traded in their F9F-7 Cougars for F11F-1 Tigers. In November, the squadron was the first to take Tigers to sea when they operated off USS *Ranger* (CV-61).

Prior to deployment with their Tigers, plans were made to give the squadron a total change of mission. As part of a modernization program of air group composition and training in 1958, VF-21 was made a part of Carrier Air Group Four (RCVG-4) and given the role of F11F transition training as a RAG.

In November 1958, the F11F Tigers were supplanted by A4D Skyhawks. The Skyhawk training assumed precedence, since the Tiger was being phased out of service. The squadron added F9F-8T Cougar, T-33B Shooting Star, and T-28B Trojan aircraft to their inventory and provid-

ed all-weather instrument ground and flight training because the majority of tactical aviation was transitioning from prop to jet aircraft, and emphasis on night and all-weather operations increased.

In July of 1959, the squadron was redesignated VA-43 in light of their switch to an attack-training mission. By 1963, their inventory included A-4C Skyhawks and TF-9J and RF-9J Cougars.

The renaissance in ACM training that came out of the Ault Report in 1968 resulted in the squadron flying occasional Adversary missions in 1970. By this time, the squadron's primary role was instrument ground school, flight training, and requalification. The Adversary mission was added officially in 1973 when the squadron was redesignated VF-43. A supersonic T-38 Talon was inherited from Topgun in 1975, and four F-5E Tigers were added in 1976. A camouflage paint scheme was introduced to the squadron aircraft, marking it as an official Adversary outfit. The squadron modified its insignia to include a smashed MiG fighter clenched by the mailed glove.

Gradually the Adversary role began to assume more importance than instrument training, and in 1978 the squadron's mission became pri-

VA-43 evolved from a fleet F9F squadron into the A-4 RAG at Oceana. VA-43 was an instrument RAG when the need for dissimilar Adversaries was recognized. The squadron was redesignated VF-43 in 1973 and acquired better performing A-4E Skyhawks for its Adversary mission. VF-43 acquired a T-38 in 1975 and three F-5E Tigers in 1976. The squadron then adopted the highly appropriate call sign of Ambush. In 1979, the squadron's TA-4Js still retained standard Navy paint schemes, as shown here. Stephen Miller via Rick Burgess

Because of concern over mishaps involving ACM-related out-of-control flight (OCF), both VF-43 and VF-126 initiated an OCF program to annually requalify all fighter crews with an academic syllabus and following flight in a T-2C Buckeye, in which a number of departures and spins are demonstrated. The forgiving nature of the Buckeye allows the aircrews to apply recovery procedures for their particular aircraft and return the aircraft to controlled flight. VF-43 maintains three to four T-2Cs for this role. VF-43 has maintained a tradition of minimal markings over the paint scheme of mixed pale grays and blues commonly referred to as "yuk," as seen on this T-2C. Dave Parsons

Initial training in the Kfir took place in Israel in two-place Israeli Air Force Kfirs as shown here. Note the VF-43 insignia painted on the revetted wall of the aircraft shelter. The Adversary mission brought a change in the squadron design to include a MiG-21 clenched in the traditional mailed fist. LCdr. Ken Neubauer

marily Adversary support. In 1979 all instrument training responsibility passed to VA-45 at NAS Cecil Field, Florida. At the same time, out-of-control flight (OCF), or "spin training" as it was known as then, was introduced using the T-2C Buckeye.

Even though the Kfir had entered service with VF-43, the A-4 was maintained in both single and two-seat versions along with the T-2C for OCF. Bruce Trombecky

A contractual hitch involving civilian maintenance support resulted in a delay in transfer of six F-16Ns from VF-45 to VF-43. To support FFARP needs in 1988, VF-45 loaned up to three F-16s and pilots at a time to VF-43 for the duration of each FFARP. Bruce Trombecky

The squadron pioneered FFARP (Fleet Fighter ACM Readiness Program), an intensive three-week syllabus that includes a series of lectures followed by dissimilar ACM flights, which became standard for all fighter

The A-4 continues to serve alongside the F-16 in the Adversary role and will stay in service until transfer of VF-43's role to VFC-12 in 1994, when VF-43 will stand down. Bob Lawson

The VF-43 flight line boasts a mix of A-4E, A-4F, and A-4F Super Fox, as well as the returning F-16Ns captured here in 1990. Dave Parsons

squadrons on both coasts. This program was initiated in 1978 and is now a part of every fleet F-14 squadron's turnaround training cycle.

In 1985, the Squadron gave up its F-5Es and received Israeli F-21A Kfirs. The Kfirs were stood down in April 1988 as the squadron awaited delivery of the F-16N Falcon. The squadron began using the Falcon in June 1988 on loan from VF-45. By 1989, VF-43 had F-16N aircraft of its own, and by the end of the year, the F-5E Tiger returned to VF-43 as well, giving the squadron a variety of dissimilar aircraft. The squadron is never without "customers" and performs a crucial role in keeping F-14 aircrews honed to a high state of readiness in ACM. In 1994, however, budgetary considerations will force the squadron to give up the role it forged on the east coast when it disestablishes and turns over responsibility for FFARP to VFC-12.

The wayward original Navy F-5Es returned to VF-43 to augment the F-16N's supersonic mission in 1991. The Navy F-5Es have a "shark" nose that provides better lift at high angles of attack. Air Force F-5Es have conical noses optimized for radar performance (Air Force F-5Es have radar, whereas the Navy F-5Es do not). Dave Parsons

Chapter 7

VF-45 Blackbirds

VF-45 is stationed at NAS Key West, Florida. The original squadron dates back to World War II when it was established as the VT-75 Black Knights, who initially flew the TBM Avenger torpedo bomber. The squadron then flew the SB2C Helldiver before transitioning to the AD-1 Skyraider in 1946 and being redesignated VA-4B.

In 1948, the squadron was redesignated again when it became VA-45 and changed its name to Blackbirds during a deployment to the Mediterranean in 1951 aboard the USS *Oriskany*. The squadron adopted an insignia featuring a cocky, cigar-smoking blackbird wearing a green derby and sporting a pair of boxing gloves along with the slogan "4 and 20." The "4 and 20" represented the original twenty-four pilots assigned to the squadron that were composed of four regular and twenty reserve pilots which happened to mimic the children's nursery rhyme of "Four and Twenty Blackbirds." The squadron held that the blackbird was chosen because of its recognized persistence and

VF-45 Skyhawk lineup at NAS Key West in 1989 shows single- and two-seat variants and a variety of paint schemes. Dave Parsons

aggressive nature in attacking and outwitting its enemies.

The Blackbirds compiled an outstanding record during the Korean War, flying 387 combat missions, dropping 1,500,000 pounds of ordnance, and losing only one aircraft in combat. After the Korean deployment, the squadron returned to NAS Jacksonville, Florida, and made subsequent deployments to the Med before disestablishment in March 1958.

Under the latest realignment of squadrons in the beginning of the sixties, which included establishment of Master Jet Bases and RAGs, VA-45 was reestablished on 15 February 1963 as the East Coast A-1H RAG at NAS Jacksonville.

In April of 1964, the squadron moved a few miles west to NAS Cecil Field and traded in its Skyraiders for TF-9J Cougars. The squadron was assigned the mission of jet instrument training, becoming a so-called instrument RAG. In March 1967, the squadron traded its Cougars for TA-4J Skyhawks. According to Capt. Rosario "Zip" Rausa, who was assigned to the Blackbirds in 1968, "Those we trained were already designated naval aviators en route to squadrons from the training command, or fleet-experienced flyers satisfying annual instrument requirements."

A Blackbird pilot preflights a VF-45 F-16N prior to an Adversary mission. The red stars on the tails caused a stir in 1992 when a senior admiral (non-aviator) passing through Key West saw the rows of VF-45 aircraft with red stars on the tails. He wanted to know why Navy aircraft were sporting red stars and directed that they be removed immediately. Dave Parsons

The squadron was once VA-45 and assumed the instrument training role after successively being a fleet attack squadron and RAG equipped with A-1H Skyraiders. In 1984, the squadron inherited the three A-4E Skyhawks previously used by VF-171's Key West ACM detachment, which was disestablished that year. The paint scheme is a "Boca Chica" design used by the detachment over the mottled blues of the numerous reefs in the operating areas near their base at Key West. VF-45 is affectionately called the Boca Chica Bogeys. Later the squadron modified the designs. Rick Burgess

The squadron mission was expanded by 1970 to include a seagoing role by providing detachments of A-4C Skyhawks. The initial detachment of five A-4C aircraft aboard USS Intrepid was increased to sixteen A-4E aircraft for a November 1972 to May 1973 deployment.

On 16 August 1976, the squadron was authorized to begin officially providing dissimilar ACM training. To mark the addition of this mission, the squadron painted two aircraft in threat camouflage paint schemes. The Adversary role continued to take on an increased percentage of the squadron's flying hours until it became their primary focus. With the standing down of RA-5 squadrons at NAS Key West and reduced role of instrument training to the point where no flights were required to support instrument training, only classroom work, the squadron moved to the clear skies of Key West, ideal for ACM.

The A-4E was added to the squadron inventory when VF-171's Key West ACM detachment stood down in June of 1984. In recognition of their virtual full-time Adversary mission, the squadron was redesignated VF-45 on 6 February 1985 and made its first detachment as VF-45 in March in support of Carrier Air Wing One (CVW-1) at NAS Fallon.

The arrival of the new F/A-18 strike fighter at NAS Cecil Field increased the demand for Adversary services. VF-45 developed the SFARP (Strike Fighter ACM Readiness Program) patterned after the F-14 community's successful FFARP program.

In 1987, VF-45 became the first and only East Coast Adversary squadron to fly the F-16N. By 1989, the squadron had eight A-4E and four TA-4J Skyhawks, and ten F-16N and two TF-16N Falcons. The squadron supported not only the burgeoning Hornet community at NAS Cecil Field, but the NAS Oceana Tomcats as well.

With the departure of the F-21A Kfir from VF-43 in 1988, VF-45 loaned F-16N aircraft to VF-43 until modifications to the civilian support contract allowed transfer of six F-16Ns to Oceana on a permanent basis. To help make up for the loss of a substantial number of supersonic assets, VF-45 re-

VF-45 began operating the F-16N in 1987 after the Navy started receiving two a month beginning in April. After the West Coast squadrons received sufficient F-16Ns, VF-45 got their first F-16Ns in October. Eventually twelve were received, making VF-45 the largest user of the F-16N before it transferred six to VF-43 in 1989. Dave Parsons

Before an Adversary pilot can fly dissimilar missions against a "customer," he must fly the entire syllabus against instructors and undergo rigorous debriefing on his airmanship as a bogey driver and, critically, his briefing and debriefing performance. Here a pilot undergoing upgrade (standing) and giving a debrief on a on-versus-two SFARP training hop listens as the operations officer gives him some pointers. Dave Parsons

The squadron operates the venerable A-4E Skyhawk alongside the F-16 to provide a mix of Adversary types. VF-101, the East Coast F-14 Tomcat RAG, frequently conducts its tactics phase at Key West to take advantage of the superb weather and VF-45 as adversaries to efficiently complete an

intensive series of dissimilar hops required by the syllabus. In supporting RAG students from VF-101, VF-174, and VFA-106, the F-16 is too hot an Adversary for the initial dissimilar hops, and the A-4E is far better for students to cut their teeth on. Michael Grove

ceived F-5E Tigers in December of 1989.

VF-101, the East Coast F-14 RAG, based at Oceana, frequently brought its Tomcats to Key West for the tactics and gunnery phases of RAG training to take advantage of the beautiful weather and Adversary aircraft. Some VF-101 instructors were cross-trained in the Skyhawk, and VF-45 made aircraft available for their use.

The squadron's ability to provide first class Adversary services was enhanced in 1990 when a joint Navy–Air Force TACTS (tactical aircrew combat training system) range became operational in the Florida keys with a display and debriefing site located adjacent to the VF-45 hangar. The squadron's primary role in the Adversary community saved it from the 1994 budget cuts, which call for VF-43 and VF-126 to stand down.

To replace the loss of six F-16Ns, the squadron received F-5Es made available by the closing down of Air Force Aggressor units and transition to the F-16 by the re-

maining squadrons. These F-5Es still wear their Air Force Aggressor paint schemes. George Hall/Check Six

Chapter 8

VF-126 Bandits

VF-126 was established on 6 April 1956 as VA-126 and equipped with F7U-3 Cutlasses. Soon after, the squadron transitioned to the F9F-8B Cougar and then the FJ-4B Fury. With the initiation of the RAG concept in 1958, VA-126 retained its FJ-4 Furies, acquired a few ADs, and then, as was common in the fifties, the squadron transitioned yet again and picked up the A4D Skyhawk in late 1958 and the role of instrument training and RAG for the A4D-1, -5, -6, and -7.

In 1961, it acquired the F9F-8T which became the standard instrument-training aircraft equipped with a collapsible hood in the rear cockpit so the student could not see out of the canopy and had to fly on instruments-only.

The squadron formed Detachment Alpha at NAS Lemoore, California, in 1961, and the detachment became the VA-127 shortly thereafter.

VA-126 was redesignated VF-126 in October 1965 and traded in its F9F

The entrance to VF-126 squadron spaces at NAS Miramar leaves no doubt as to the mission of the squadron. After the Adversary mission became predominant, the squadron modified its insignia to the red star with A-4 superimposed, as seen here. Dave Parsons

Cougars for TA-4F Skyhawks in early 1967. These Skyhawks figured prominently in the initial days of Topgun when they were used on a routine basis by instructors from VF-121 for dissimilar ACM training.

VF-126 became responsible for OCF (out-of-control flight) training for the West Coast squadrons in 1978 and maintained several T-2C Buckeyes especially configured for this task. That same year, the first high-powered A-4F Super Fox Adversary aircraft arrived at VF-126, giving the squadron a deadly "knife fighter" that posed a difficult challenge to the F-14 at slower speeds and deprived it of the energy sanctuary it enjoyed while fighting the lower-powered TA-4J and A-4E Skyhawks.

To increase fleet ACM readiness, the squadron developed TAP (Turnaround ACM Program) in December of 1980, which involved two days of lectures followed by a series of dissimilar ACM over a two-week period. One-versus-one, two-versus-one, and unknown-number-of-bogey flights were flown on the Yuma ACM range (ACMR—now called TACTS).

In 1981, the squadron changed its name to Bandits because it became a full-time Adversary unit having given instrument-training responsibility to VA-127.

The Bandits' aircraft began sporting an assortment of Adversary paint schemes. By 1982, the squadron had three A-4F Super Foxes, eleven TA-4J Skyhawks, and three T-2C Buckeyes. In 1983, VF-126 standardized its RAG ACM training with the East Coast program and conducted its first FFARP in February. FFARP included thirteen dissimilar ACM training sorties over a three-week period after two days of academics. Topgun returned the earlier favor by loaning its F-5Es to VF-126 for FFARP. In 1985, VF-126 took custody of VF-43's three F-5Es and single T-38 when VF-43 converted to the F-21A Kfir. By August of 1985, the F-5Es and T-38 were incorporated into the FFARP conducted for VF-114 and VF-213. The Bandits' aircraft were augmented by "guest" adversaries from VX-4 flying three F/A-18 Hornets.

The CO of VF-126 in 1985 was none other than Cdr. Randy "Duke" Cunningham, the first ace in Vietnam, who credited his fifth victory over a very talented opponent to the lessons learned from fighting Lt. Dave Frost in a VF-126 TA-4J during the early days of Topgun. The TA-4Js were progressively swapped for more capable A-4E and A-4F Skyhawks. In April 1987, the squadron began receiving the F-16N, which gave the Adversary

community the first aircraft capable of simulating the thrust-to-weight ratio, turning performance, and superior radar of such fourth-generation threat aircraft as the MiG-29, Su-27, and Mirage 2000.

Unfortunately, a VF-126 A-4E was lost with its pilot in 1992, precipitating the withdrawal of all A-4Es from the Adversary program. Cdr. John "Bug" Roach was lost when his ejection seat failed to function properly. The loss of the A-4E was mitigated by availability of A-4M Skyhawks, with performance comparable to that of the A-4F Super Fox, which had been declared excess by the Marine Corps reserve. Current plans call for eventual retirement of the A-4 from Adversary service as early as fiscal year 1994.

Cost concerns have resulted in the decision to close down VF-126 in 1994. Responsibility of supporting the West Coast Tomcat community will pass to VFC-13, which will transition to the F/A-18 Hornet and give up its Skyhawks.

No other squadron can claim such a primary role in shaping the renais-

This A-4F seen in 1983 features a matching top and bottom paint scheme with a fake cockpit, including helmet, painted on the lower fuselage. This has been adopted by different units, including Canadians, in hopes it will fool an opponent's perception as to which way the aircraft is turning, which might force an error or cause hesitation. Michael Grove

When VF-43 received its Kfirs in 1985, VF-126 acquired VF-43's three F-5Es and single T-38, shown here in 1987. D. F. Brown

As the supply of A-4Es and A-4Fs dwindled and supply support became an increasingly difficult proposition, the A-4M was introduced as an Adversary. It has the same J52-408 engine that makes the A-4F Super Fox so potent, but slightly less thrust-to-weight because it is heavier and has more drag. This "Mike" sports VF-126 colors in 1988. VF-126 will stand down, and the Skyhawk will be retired from Adversary duty at the end of fiscal year 1993, marking twenty-five years of valued service right up to the end, since Topgun first borrowed VF-126 Skyhawks for dissimilar ACM. Michael Grove

sance in fighter training brought about in 1968. The VF-126 Bandits will be dearly missed by all who ever had the occasion to meet them in the air, and certainly those who used the call sign.

With the dissolution of the Soviet Union, the red star seems slightly out of place as the symbol of the Adversary, so the red stars on VF-126 aircraft were replaced in late 1991 by miniature flags of countries with less-than-friendly relations with the United States, as shown on this A-4F at NAS Fallon. Michael Grove

Chapter 9

VFA-127 Desert Bogeys

The VFA-127 Desert Bogeys were originally a detachment of VF-126 formed to provide the core of a jet instrument training unit at NAS Lemoore, California. An advance party of one officer and seventeen enlisted personnel from VF-126, the RAG component of RCVG-12, equipped with the F9F-8T, arrived at newly commissioned NAS Lemoore on 12 July 1961. On July 24, the unit was designated Detachment Alpha and became the first unit to fly scheduled flights out of Lemoore. Detachment Alpha provided instrument RAG training for the wing's pilots. Equipped with F9F-8T (TF-9J as of 1 September 1962) Cougars, the unit also provided transition training and refresher training in the Cougar. On 15 June 1962, the unit ceased being a detachment and was established as VA-127, as part of

RCVG-12, the parent command for West Coast RAGs.

VA-127 flew the Cougar until September 1966 when the TA-4J Skyhawk arrived. In May 1970, the squadron became the RAG for the A-4, serving in this role until July of 1975. In November of the same year, the squadron became officially tasked with

providing dissimilar ACM training in addition to its instrument RAG duties. Both dissimilar ACM training and instrument training continued, with dissimilar ACM training gradually becoming the primary focus of the unit. Camouflage paint schemes began to adorn the squadron aircraft to denote the Adversary mission, although fleet

Two VFA-127 Hornets fly in formation over the Nevada mountains near their home base at NAS Fallon. The F/A-18A Hornet Adversary paint scheme features the outline of a MiG-29 superimposed on the Hornet. The Hornet will also be introduced as the primary Adversary at NAS Miramar with VFC-13 and at NAS Oceana with VFC-12 when VF-126 and VF-43 close their doors in 1994. Topgun also hopes to acquire the F/A-18 as well. McDonnell Douglas via Lon Nordeen

One of the most interesting and unique paint schemes used on any Adversary plane was this MiG-17 silhouette painted on a

VA-127 TA-4J, shown as it appeared in 1983. Michael Grove

By 1982, the side-number colors were standardized red with yellow border, a common Aggressor and Adversary choice. By 1983, the squadron acquired single-seat Sky- hawks as seen here in March 1983. Michael Grove

With the arrival of the F/A-18 Hornet at NAS Lemoore in 1987, the squadron changed its designation to VFA-127 and began supporting VFA-125, the F/A-18 RAG, with dissimilar ACM training missions. The squadron acquired the bulk of F- 5Es when the F-16N arrived and it ferried seven Air Force F-5Es from England to NAS Fallon. Here a VFA-106 Hornet, the East Coast RAG, holds short for takeoff with two VFA-127 F-5Es. Robert Genat/Arms Communications

gray paint schemes were still maintained on some aircraft until the eighties. The squadron was the last of the Adversary units to acquire single-seat Skyhawks to enhance its performance as an Adversary squadron.

The Adversary mission took on added importance in 1987 with the arrival of the F/A-18 into the light-attack community. The squadron was redesignated VFA-127 and moved to nearby NAS Fallon, Nevada, in November in order to better perform its mission. Coincident with the move, the squadron acquired F-5E Tigers made available when VF-126 and Topgun received their F-16Ns. Additional F-5Es were ferried by seven VFA-127 aircrews from RAF Alconbury, England, from the Air Force's 527th Aggressor squadron in July 1988 when it transitioned to the F-16C Falcon.

NAS Fallon's growth from a bare-bones base into the Navy's Strike Warfare Center had included the first air-wing-capable TACTS range, which VFA-127 was able to take full advantage of when SFARP was introduced to the Lemoore-based Hornet squadrons in 1985.

In 1992, VFA-127 gave up its F-5Es and Skyhawks and became the first Adversary squadron to be equipped with the F/A-18A Hornet. In its superb Fallon location, where air wings from both coasts deploy as part of their work-ups prior to cruise, the squadron plays a vital role as home-field Adversary, a duty that comprises one-third of the squadron's missions. Another third is devoted to supporting VFA-125, the West Coast F/A-18 RAG, with SFARP. Half of the remaining missions are flown in SFARP sorties for Lemoore-based Hornets and the other half on in-house training and other missions.

An unusual black paint scheme appeared on this VFA-127 F-5E in May of 1989 at NAS Fallon, perhaps influenced by the Top Gun *movie paint scheme.* Michael Grove

VFA-127 was the first squadron to operate the F/A-18A Hornet as an Adversary. The Hornet was introduced in 1992 and has been found to be extremely successful. The stripped A-model Hornets are actually dissimilar enough to present a dissimilar op- *ponent for the F/A-18C Hornets flying with external stores.* Michael Grove

Chapter 10

VFC-12 Fighting Omars

The VFC-12 Fighting Omars were established at NAF Detroit, Michigan as Composite Squadron Twelve (VC-12) on 1 September 1973 making the unit the first reserve fleet composite squadron in Naval Aviation history (along with VC-13 which was established on the same day). The squadron moved to NAS Oceana, Virginia, in June 1975 with its A-4L Skyhawks augmenting the fleet support provided there by the active-duty VC-2 Blue Falcons. VC-2 was disestablished in the fall of 1980, leaving VC-12 as the sole fleet support squadron on the East Coast.

The squadron's continual series of detachments supporting both active and reserve units led to the unofficial squadron nickname of the "Home of the Road Gang" which is particularly apropos in light of 1988's record of twenty-six detachments totaling 190 days.

In 1988, the squadron was redesignated VFC-12 reflecting its primary role as an Adversary squadron flying fighter missions. In its day-to-day role, the squadron flies dissimilar ACM training with fleet Tomcat squadrons and supports the dissimilar ACM training requirements of VF-101's tactics syllabus as well as towing air-to-air gunnery banners for both. Additionally, the squadron performs the traditional composite mission of radar-tracking hops for ships' training, air-

VFC-12 favors the semi-gloss, almost charcoal-gray paint scheme shown here on a TA-4J taxiing at NAS Oceana. Bruce Trombecky

In 1992, VFC-12 operated an average of six A-4F (five Super Fox and one "straight") along with six TA-4J Models. The squadron has maintained a reputation for immaculate appearance of its aircraft. The semi-gloss gray allows for easier corrosion work, as the flat paints used on most Navy aircraft fade quicker, and corrosion spot paint makes them look splotchy. Dave Parsons

VC-12 operated the TA-4J as a fleet services platform towing gunnery banners and flying other ship's services missions such as air-intercept-controller training. The squadron eventually acquired the role of dissimilar ACM training, supplementing VF-43. A large percentage of VC-12 Adversary pilots come from VF-43 and are qualified Adversary instructors. US Navy

VFC-12 is frequently on the road giving rise to the name "Road Gang" as detachments of one to six aircraft are constantly in demand to support fleet and reserve units all over the country. Here a VFC-12 A-4F taxis at NAS Oceana. Garry English

intercept control, and target towing for surface ships. The squadron is well suited to provide Adversary services because, routinely, almost three-quarters of the seven active duty reserve and 33 reserve officers come from Adversary instructor backgrounds. Many pilots come directly off active duty with VF-43 into VFC-12, bringing their expertise with them.

The squadron will become NAS Oceana's sole Adversary asset in 1994 when VF-43 is disestablished and VFC-12 gives up its Skyhawks and transitions to the F/A-18A Hornet. In order to provide continuity and enhance the squadron's new role in providing FFARP, the squadron will have active-duty aviators assigned as well as active-duty and part-time reservists.

A VFC-12 A-4F Super Fox joins the VF-45 Skyhawk flight line at NAS Key West. The squadron is a frequent visitor to Key West, supporting VF-101 detachments as well as VFA-106 and fleet squadrons. Dave Parsons

Chapter 11

VFC-13 Saints

VFC-13 was established at NAS New Orleans on 1 September 1973. Initially designated VC-13, the squadron was equipped with F-8H Crusaders and manned by seventeen officers and 127 enlisted personnel drawn from former members of disestablished Antisubmarine Fighter Squadrons Seventy-six and Eighty-six (VSF-76 and VSF-86).

In April 1974, the squadron began transitioning to the A-4L Skyhawk. The composite squadron mission required the squadron to provide fleet support that entailed target towing for surface-to-air gunnery and missile training, and for air-to-air gunnery as well as flights for air-intercept-controller training. Demand for target-towing services on the West Coast brought a move to NAS Miramar in February 1976 to augment the A-4Fs and TA-4Js of the VC-7 Red Tails. In the fall of 1976, the A-4Ls were traded in for TA-4J models increasing the squadron's flexibility. VC-7 was disestablished on 1 October 1980 leaving

The introduction of the A-4F Super Fox gave VFC-13 a potent Adversary aircraft with its greater than 1:1 thrust ratio at lower fuel states. Here a Super Fox climbs vertically off the coast of Southern California. Bob Lawson

VC-13 as the sole composite unit serving the West Coast.

Following the instrument RAG entry into officially sanctioned ACM, increased demand for dissimilar ACM

training resulted in VC-13 flying Adversary missions in addition to fleet support. In 1983, the squadron received A-4E Skyhawks to augment their TA-4Js and strengthen their ca-

VC-13 was equipped with the A-4L Skyhawk when it moved from NAS New Orleans to NAS Miramar. The squadron later transitioned to the TA-4J. via Rick Burgess

pability as Adversaries. Later, the vaunted A-4F Super Fox arrived, and by 1989, the squadron operated seven TA-4J Skyhawks and seven A-4F Super Foxes. The preponderance of ACM as a squadron mission brought about a redesignation to VFC-13. The squadron has been continually active supporting both Carrier Air Wing Reserve Thirty (CAWR-30) and fleet squadrons at Miramar with dissimilar ACM adversaries. Many of the

VC-13 TA-4J Skyhawk in 1979 bears twelve silhouettes denoting success over the F-4 in ACM. VC-13's move to NAS Mira- *mar in the seventies brought composite services to the Pacific Fleet. VC-13 supported VF-301 and VF-302 with Adversary ser-* *vices and filled in for the fleet when VF-126 or Topgun were unavailable. Rick Burgess*

The popularity of dissimilar ACM training missions and increased demand brought *low visibility paint schemes to the squadron, as seen here in 1981 as a TA-4J* *taxis at Fallon in support of a weapons detachment. Michael Grove*

Reserve Tomcat squadrons VF-301 and 302 are co-located with VFC-13 at NAS Miramar and conduct dissimilar ACM training with each other frequently. Here a VFC-13 A-4F Super Fox returns to Miramar with two VF-301 Tomcats in 1989. Bob Lawson

squadron's requests involve detachments to bases all over the country keeping the Saints on the road constantly.

In 1992, the budgetary decisions to consolidate the Adversary community resulted in the selection of VFC-13 to remain as the sole Adversary unit at NAS Miramar when VF-126 is disestablished in 1994. At that time, VFC-13 will transition to the F/A-18A Hornet and say farewell to the Skyhawk.

Two VFC-13 Super Foxes taxi to the runway with spoilers armed. The squadron will operate the Super Fox until late 1993 when it begins transition to the F/A-18A Hornet and takes the place of VF-126, which will disband, leaving VFC-13 as Miramar's sole Adversary squadron. Robert Genat/Arms Communications

Chapter 12

VMFT-401 Snipers

VMFT-401 is the most recent addition to the Navy and Marine Corps Adversary community and the first dedicated adversary squadron in the Marine Corps. The squadron was established on 18 March 1986 as a reserve squadron, it serves the many active-duty Marine Corps units based at or visiting MCAS Yuma. The squadron was formed to take advantage of a second offer from the government of Israel to lease Kfir fighters on a no cost-basis (excluding maintenance and operating costs). The first contingent of five F-21A Kfirs arrived at Yuma on 25 June 1987. The initial cadre of pilots assembled in 1986 spent the intervening time training with VF-43 at NAS Oceana (who had received their Kfirs in 1985) and receiving a brief familiarization course in Israel. By the end of 1987, all thirteen Kfirs had arrived at Yuma and were pressed into service. The squadron flew the Kfir extensively until their transfer to NAS Norfolk on 22 September 1989 to await shipment back to Israel. The

The Marine Adversary tail insignia features a Marine Corps symbol superimposed on a Red Star. The bureau number indicated that this is one of the original Navy F-5Es that have seen service in several Adversary squadrons. Bob Lawson

An F-21A Kfir taxis back to the VMFT-401 flight line after an Adversary mission. Dave Parsons

squadron was extremely pleased with the Kfir flying 9,184 sorties totaling 7,892 hours while maintaining over 99 percent reliability.

In anticipation of the departure of the Kfir later that year, the squadron received its first F-5E Tigers from Nellis-based Air Force Aggressor squadron s in April. The F-5E was flown alongside the Kfir until the latter's departure.

As a primary training base and home of the Marine Aviation Weapons & Tactics Squadron One (MAWTS-1), Yuma plays host to the entire gamut of Marine aviation throughout the year and twice a year hosts the month-long MAWTS Weapons and Tactics Instructor (WTI) course. VMFT-401 is the primary source of Adversaries for these exercises alone. The squadron is staffed by seven active-duty reserve officers and ten Selected Marine Corps Reserve (SMCR) pilots, as well as associated support personnel. Although a fourth-generation adversary aircraft such as the F-16N or F/A-18 would be ideal, VMFT-401 flies a great deal of missions against attack aircraft such as the AV-8B Harrier that do not need as sophisticated an opponent as does the F/A-18 Hornet. The squadron takes full advantage of the Yuma TACTS range and supports the MCAS El Toro Hornet squadrons as well as the MCAS Yuma squadrons.

The Marines stood up their first and only Adversary squadron in 1987 at MCAS Yuma, Arizona, with thirteen Israeli F-21A Kfirs. MCAS Yuma is a central location for Marine tactical aviation due to its superb weather and vast exercise areas that are used for combined arms exercises. Roth

After two years with the Kfir, the squadron introduced the F-5E in April of 1989 and operated both types until September, when the Kfirs were returned to Israel. Bob Lawson/Check Six

VMFT-401 reserve pilots are required to live in the Yuma area because of its somewhat remote location and the need to support a very active base on a daily basis. VMFT-401 was the first reserve full-time Adversary squadron with a mission to support active-duty training. In 1994, the Navy will adopt the same idea when reserve squadrons VFC-12 and VFC-13 become the Adversary squadrons for the F-14 community. Bob Lawson

Three VMFT-401 F-5Es climb in formation over the Arizona desert. VMFT-401 supports defensive ACM training for AV-8B Harriers that are located at MCAS Yuma and those that visit the base on weapons detachments. Katsuhiko Tokunaga/Check Six

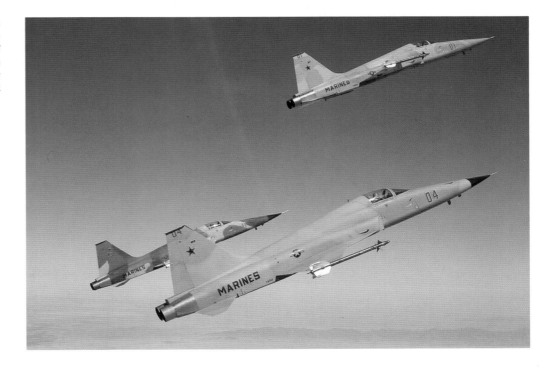

An F-5E with a Cubic Corp. TACTS pod outside the hangarettes. VMFT-401 has use of the original TACTS range, which is located at Yuma and was recently upgraded to state-of-the-art thirty-six–aircraft capability, a big change from the original four-aircraft system. Bob Lawson

VC-8 operates TA-4J Skyhawks out of NAS Roosevelt Roads, Puerto Rico, as part-time Adversaries in support of visiting carrier air wings. Dave Parsons

Chapter 13

VC-8 Red Tails

The VC-8 Red Tails trace their lineage to the Navy's first "cruise" missile, the Regulus attack missile. During the development of the Regulus, a detachment from VU-4 and Guided-Missile Unit Fifty-three (GMU-53 provided controller aircraft and missile support at the Navy's Chincoteague, Virginia, facility, arriving in late 1954. The VU-4 pilots flew two F9F-2KD Panthers and two TV-2Ds. In early 1955, F9F-6Ds were added to the stable. The two units merged on 25 September 1955 forming Guided Missile Group Two (GMGRU-2) as the Regulus concept matured. During 1956, GMGRU-2 operated detachments aboard USS Macon (CA-132), USS Randolph (CVA-15), and USS Barbero (SSG-317), a submarine especially configured with a hangar for the missile.

At that time the unit operated the Regulus with FJ-3D Fury control aircraft. The Furies were especially configured to control the Regulus from the cockpit. The missile had the option of a high-explosive or nuclear warhead. The concept called for the Fury to guide the Regulus to the vicinity of the target at which time the missile would continue on its own. This kept the pilot clear of terminal target defenses and out of the blast. Missile guidance development had not matured enough to give the missile its own inertial guidance all the way to the target. In 1958, the Regulus was abandoned and the unit was redesignated Guided Missile Service Squadron Two (GMSRON-2) on 1 July. As the Regulus faded from the scene, the squadron acquired BQM-34 Firebees, AQM-37A supersonic targets, and TDU-series towed targets.

On 15 January 1959, the squadron moved to NAS Roosevelt Roads, to provide target support for fleet units training in the Puerto Rican operating area. In July of 1969, the squadron was redesignated VU-8. After the move, the squadron continued to provide target drones for fleet training, launching forty-one drones in the six-month period from July to December 1960, which was only the beginning of high-tempo drone launches of BQM-34s and QF-9s in support of the increased numbers of missile-armed ships rapidly entering fleet service. To support its mission, the squadron acquired an assortment of aircraft in addition to its FJ-3D Furies including the DP-2 Neptune, DT-28 Trojan, UH-34 Seahorse, QF-9 Cougar, US-2C Tracker, and DF-8 Crusader.

The Atlantic Fleet Weapons Range off the coast of Puerto Rico became the primary location for Navy missile-firing exercises because of its superb weather and isolated location. The long range of surface-to-air and air-to-air missiles entering the inventory necessitated large areas of water without surface traffic in order to safely fire. The location and range facilities also were used by Canadian, British, Dutch, and Brazilian navies.

During the Cuban Missile Crisis in 1962, VC-8 was called upon to provide high-speed courier service to Guantanamo Bay, Cuba, and Washington, D.C., with its FJ Furys. The Fury couriers rushed photographs, obtained by RF-8s operating over Cuba, to eager recipients in Washington and Gitmo, flying thirty missions before the lessoning of tensions.

Another highlight of squadron history was during June 1965 when the squadron provided eighty-nine low-altitude presentations in a four-day period. In July, the squadron was redesignated VC-8. In 1967, the squadron marked the launch of the one thousandth BQM-34. The squadron then received A-4B Skyhawks to replace the aged Furies.

VC-8 eventually shed its assortment of aircraft and reduced its complement to the SH-3G Seaking helicopters and TA-4J Skyhawks. To support the fleet, these aircraft fly a wide variety of missions including drone and torpedo launch and recovery, search and rescue, VIP transport, air-controller training, air-to-air and surface-to-air gunnery banner towing. The squadron occasionally works with Guantanamo-based VC-10. In 1983, two VC-8 Skyhawks and four pilots deployed to Guantanamo Bay for one week to augment VC-10 by flying tracking exercises and towing aerial banners.

In 1986, ACM was added to the squadron's mission. Although the squadron flew fighters in its early years, ACM was not a designated mission. However, looser rules did not prevent VU-8's Crusaders, Furies, or Cougars from taking on Air Force F-86s flying out of nearby San Juan, Puerto Rico. Tightening of rules through the seventies put a halt to unrestricted ACM. When ACM was reintroduced in 1986, it was done so by the book with VC-8 pilots participating in the Navy fighter Weapons School Adversary training. Before the end of 1986, the squadron was "legally" engaging CVW-3 F-14 Tomcats, VFA-131 Hornets, RAF Buccaneers, Puerto Rican Air National Guard A-7Ds, and USAF F-4 Phantoms.

Today, VC-8 retains six TA-4J Skyhawks and their Adversary mission.

VC-8 flies a mix of TA-4J Skyhawks and SH-3 Seakings to support the Atlantic Fleet training exercises that occur almost continually in the Puerto Rican Operating Area. The squadron is authorized to conduct dissimilar ACM training in addition to its varied fleet support missions. Rick Burgess

VC-10 operates TA-4J Skyhawks out of Guantanamo Bay, Cuba, to support fleet training. This is a paint scheme used in 1980 prior to adoption of low visibility coloring. Michael Grove

Chapter 14

VC-10 Challengers

The history of VC-10 dates back to 26 October 1943 when VU-16 was established at San Juan, Puerto Rico. The squadron was assigned the mission of providing training services to the fleet in defense against airborne attack. Operating the JM (a Navy version of the Martin B-26 Marauder) the squadron moved to Miami, Florida, on 10 May 1944, only to move less than a year later to NAS Guantanamo Bay, Cuba, where it has remained ever since. On 16 August 1946, the squadron was redesignated VU-10.

Jet aircraft were added to the squadron's inventory in 1954 with the arrival of the F9F Cougar. These aircraft were used for high-speed, high-altitude air services to Atlantic Fleet ships during their work-ups in order to train air controllers, radar operators, anti-aircraft weapon system operators, and combat information center (CIC) personnel. The Cougar was replaced during 1958 by the FJ-3 Fury.

As relations with Cuba deteriorated in the early sixties, the squadron was assigned the additional mission of air support for defense of the US presence at Guantanamo Bay. To provide additional capability against the Soviet-supplied MiGs, the squadron added the F-8 Crusader to its inventory. This brought about a change to the squadron insignia in the form of a crusader's cross on a shield. During the Cuban Missile Crisis in October of 1962, the Crusaders maintained around-the-clock combat air patrol (CAP) over the base.

The squadron was redesignated VC-10 in July 1965 and adopted the call sign of Challengers in 1969. The squadron insignia was changed again in 1972 to the current design featuring a black fighting lion on a field of red, white, and blue.

The Squadron began transitioning from the Crusader to the TA-4J Skyhawk in 1976. The Skyhawks continued to perform the mission of air defense for the base and were equipped for both air-to-air and air-to-surface weapons. VC-10 remains the only TA-4J squadron configured for the AIM-9 Sidewinder. In addition to their fleet support missions, the squadron expends over 150 tons of ordnance annually to maintain readiness. Nine combat configured TA-4J and one EA-4F Skyhawks make up today's complement of aircraft.

The squadron sends Adversary detachments to other locations to support fleet exercises and individual units. Pilots are routinely sent to the

VC-10 is unique in having a combat mission in addition to fleet support and dissimilar ACM training missions. VC-10 Skyhawks are configured to carry external stores, as seen here carrying a mix of Rockeye bombs and AIM-9 Sidewinder missiles. Working in a Communist country every day forces the squadron to be able to defend its base if needed. US Navy

Adversary Course at Navy Fighter Weapons School (Topgun) in order to maintain qualified ACM pilots. This serves to allow VC-10 to be a more professional Adversary and increases readiness for their "real-world" air-to-air mission. The squadron often provides detachments to NAS Roosevelt Roads to augment and support the TA-4J Skyhawks of VC-8.

Index